Dragonflies of the Colorado Front Range

A Photographic Guide

Ann Cooper

Boulder County Nature Association
Boulder, Colorado
2014

Copyright © 2014 Ann Cooper

Editor: Lysa Wegman-French

Design and Layout: George Oetzel

Photo Editors: Stephen R. Jones and Sharon Daugherty

Illustrations: Amy Chu

Cover Design: Jim Primock and Sharon Daugherty

Cover photo: Halloween Pennant female, Ann Cooper

Back cover photos: Twelve-spotted Skimmer male (left) and Boreal Bluet pair (right), Ann Cooper

Title page photo: Calico Pennant male, Richard Holmes

Interior photos:

John S. Barr 8, 10, 34, 40, 47, 72, 74, 75, 93. Ann Cooper 7, 10, 13, 21, 23, 25, 27, 28, 31, 33, 35, 37, 38, 42, 46, 51, 52, 56, 61, 62, 63, 64, 65, 66, 69, 73, 76, 78, 79, 87, 91, 92, 95, 96, 97, 98. Leslie Flint 49, 54, 58. Richard Holmes 22, 36, 39, 40, 41, 51, 53, 57, 59, 60, 62, 64, 71, 82, 85, 90. Jim Johnson 19, 23, 80, 83. Stephen R. Jones 9, 14, 41, 43, 45, 55, 59, 69, 81, 88, 89, 92. Leslie Larson 24, 27, 32, 65, 71, 84, 86. Bill Maynard 63. Celeste Mazzacano/Xerces Society 20, 30. Jeff Mitton 53. Inez Prather 48, 50. Scott E. Severs 94.

ISBN 978-0-9837020-1-6

Boulder County Nature Association,
P.O. Box 493, Boulder, Colorado 80306
http://www.bcna.org

CONTENTS

ACKNOWLEDGMENTS

I wish to thank:

The Ted Hughes Estate for permission to use an excerpt from the poem "Dragonfly."

Dennis Paulson, for permission to use his numbers for the dragonfly and damselfly sizes.

Bill Prather, for reviewing both the manuscript and the photographs, and for patiently answering my many questions.

Scott Severs, for first introducing me to the world of dragonflies and damselflies.

My friends in the Boulder County Nature Association who all had a hand in producing this book: George Oetzel, Steve Jones, Lysa Wegman-French, Sharon Daugherty, and Amy Chu.

Boulder County Parks and Open Space for granting yearly catch-and-release permits for their properties so I could meet the local dragonflies up close.

INTRODUCTION

Ted Hughes: "Dragonfly"

from *The Cat and the Cuckoo*, Sunstone Press, 1987.

Dragonflies are the very essence of summer. Watch them dart over ponds and clearings as they hunt for prey—forward, backward, up, down, hovering, turning on a dime. In their shimmering, rainbow colors, how can they fail to catch the eye as they zip past?

Having caught the eye, what then? Many people want to know more. What kind are they? How can you tell? What are they doing when they fly in pairs, or form heart-shaped wheels?

There's no shortage of excellent and comprehensive field guides that offer this information. But for anyone newly interested in this hobby, the information overload can be mind boggling. This book attempts to limit the overwhelming information by showcasing the species most likely to be seen in the Front Range area.

Dragonfly watching—oding, as it's sometimes called (from Odonata, the name of this order of insects)—is a relatively new outdoor pastime. Once, it was hard to identify an individual unless you netted it, and manuals were highly technical. Close-focus binoculars, digital cameras, and photographic field guides have changed that. With these tools, it's possible to identify many (though not all) species without catching them. As a result, many people who once focused on birds or butterflies now watch dragonflies as well. As you might expect, with all these extra eyes looking we're learning all the time.

Which raises the question, should you catch dragonflies and damselflies? That is a personal choice. You can catch them to study and identify, then release them unharmed, but be aware that a permit is often required. Be sure to know the regulations. Dragonflies should be collected only if there is a valid scientific reason to do so, and if the specimens will become part of an accredited collection.

Why is it important to know which dragonflies live here, and where they live? Apart from the obvious reasons—that they are amazing insects bringing endless delight—dragonflies are a vital part of all aquatic ecosystems, key players in food chains and in the balance of species around ponds and marshes. Selfishly, we might welcome them for all the biting insects they eat. We should also be grateful when ponds are teeming with a variety of dragonfly species, for it suggests those wetlands are in a healthy state.

Geographic Scope

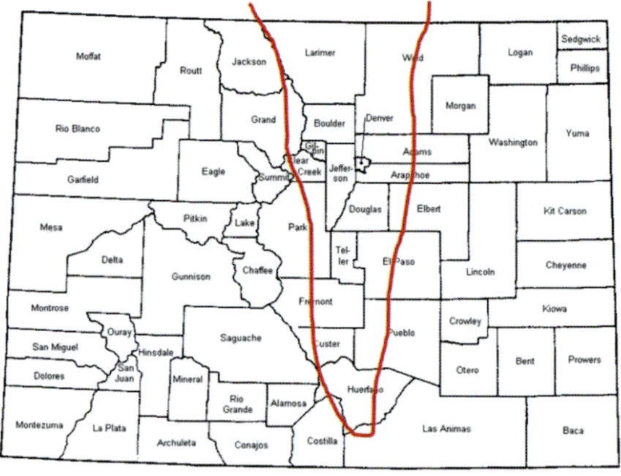

This book covers the most common species that occur in the area inside the red "V" on the Colorado map, but does not claim to include everything you might see. There's much to learn. The dragonflies of the counties included are not equally well studied. For example, more species have been documented in Larimer and Boulder counties simply because more people have looked there for dragonflies over the years. There are other gaps in our knowledge of dragonflies in the Front Range, too. The flight season of some high elevation species is not precisely known. In addition, information on species living in particular life zones is often extrapolated from records amassed in other states, rather than from local records. For all these reasons, information gleaned by pursuing this fascinating hobby can turn into citizen science of measurable value.

The topographic area covered in this book spans many life zones from grasslands and foothills, to the montane, subalpine and alpine. Some species are limited to particular life zones and habitats, while others are generalists and likely to be seen over a wider range of habitats. Researchers have not yet learned these characteristics for all Front Range species.

Several species of dragonfly migrate, although the details of such journeys are only now being studied. At certain times of year, you may see large numbers of dragonflies traveling in the same direction together. If you are lucky enough to see this, please report it to the Migratory Dragonfly Partnership (see Groups on page 101).

Ecology & Life Cycle

Dragonflies begin life as eggs laid in the water of ponds, swamps, puddles, rivers, ditches, stock tanks, rain barrels, wet bogs, meadows, and all such watery places. The eggs hatch into larvae that live in the water, eating voraciously and growing apace. They are fierce predators of small insects, fish, and tadpoles. Like all insects, they have exoskeletons (hard outside shells) and must molt (shed) them when the larvae need to grow. The larvae undergo a long series of molts in the water before they are ready to emerge as dragonflies. This larval stage can take from weeks or months to many years (in cold, high elevation lakes). There is no stage in a dragonfly's life equivalent to the butterfly pupa—dragonflies are said to undergo "incomplete metamorphosis."

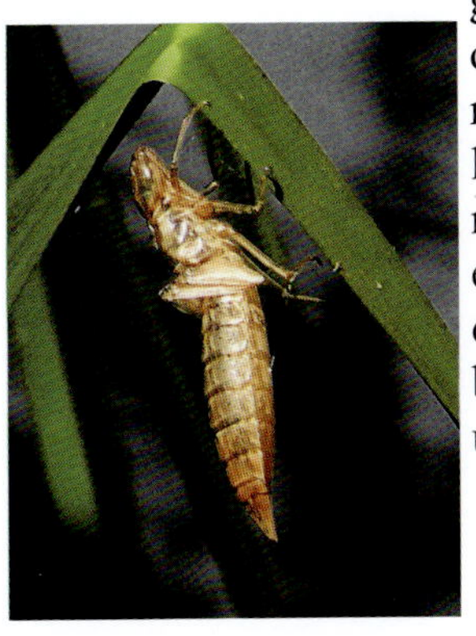

Exuvia, or hatch case, left by an emerged dragonfly

When the dragonfly is ready to emerge, the larva, sometimes called a nymph, stops eating. It stops using gills to breathe, and starts using air holes (spiracles) to breathe on land. The larva crawls out of the water on a handy stem, twig, or rock. It cracks out of its last too-tight shell, leaving the husk (exuvia) of its previous life behind. You can often find these shells still clinging to reeds on which larvae crawled to emerge.

The wings un-crumple as hemolymph (bug blood) flows into the wing veins. Gradually the wings fully extend and dry, and then the "teneral," or just-hatched dragonfly, is able to fly weakly. Over the next hours and days the insect becomes a stronger flier and develops full color.

New adult dragonflies often stay away from the water, resting and feeding in grasslands or woodland edges for variable lengths of time (days or weeks) until they become sexually mature. You may see them singly, or in large feeding swarms, well away from water.

When dragonflies become sexually mature, they return to wetlands to meet and mate. You may see "mating wheels" when pairs are copulating. The male grabs the female behind her head with his cerci (see page 13). The female uses her abdomen tip to collect sperm from where the male previously placed it under segments 2 and 3 of his abdomen—thus, the wheel. You may see tandem pairs, when males and females are preparing to go into the wheel, or when the females are ready to lay eggs. Males may stay in tandem to "contact guard" their mates—and ensure their paternity. Some dragonflies are scattershot egg layers, dropping eggs as they fly over the water or dipping the abdomen

Brightly colored male on the top with the female below.

repeatedly at the water surface. Others inject their eggs into wetland plants and may go underwater to do so. With egg laying, the whole life cycle starts again.

A tandem pair of bluets—getting ready to mate, or preparing to lay eggs. The male (left) grasps the female behind her head with his cerci.

Names and Classification

Up until now, we've used the term "dragonfly" as shorthand to include both dragonflies and damselflies (scientists and naturalists commonly do this). Dragonfly in this context includes all insects in the scientific order Odonata ("toothed jaws"). The order Odonata is divided into two main subgroups: the dragonflies, Anisoptera ("differently shaped wings"), and the damselflies, Zygoptera ("same-shaped wings"). This book includes species from both groups. The true dragonflies, Anisoptera, are larger, often the first odonates to attract people's attention, and more easily studied and photographed. For that reason, they are discussed first in this book. Many of the damselflies are not possible to tell apart without netting them and inspecting tiny anatomical details, which is beyond the scope of this book. Dragonflies and damselflies have two-part scientific names, and also highly descriptive and memorable standardized common names. Both scientific and common names are given in this book.

Typical dragonfly — Variegated Meadowhawk

Typical damselfly — Plains Forktail

Conservation

What most influences the survival of dragonflies? It's the old, old story—habitat. Dragonflies need natural wetlands in order to thrive. Agricultural runoff, the use of pesticides, and dredging and draining of wetlands all take their toll on local dragonfly populations.

As with many understudied animals, we are likely to lose dragonfly species before we even know of their importance. Any contribution made towards understanding the complete environmental needs of dragonfly species is vital to ensuring that these insects stay around for the long haul.

Fortunately, individual species don't usually need that much room in order to thrive. Even a sunny garden pond can contribute to overall habitat for dragonflies and provide a great opportunity to watch and learn as these wondrous creatures go about their lives.

When it comes to global climate change, we don't know if, or how, the weather patterns in various areas will change in the coming years. Severe droughts that eliminate wetlands in whole regions will no doubt impact dragonfly species. After all, they do need watery habitats for much of their life cycle. And although they are capable of dispersing to new wetland areas, there's a limit to the distances that many of them can travel to find new homes.

Watching and Photographing

Watching dragonflies is a lot like watching other wildlife. Make yourself inconspicuous and take your time.

- Be sneaky. Approach a perched dragonfly from directly behind, because that's where its vision is the least sensitive. Move very slowly. Avoid tangling with vegetation that can shake the insect's perch. It is possible to get very close by stealth.

- Be slow. Sit still on a pond bank and wait for the action to come to you. Even after an insect flies away, patience could pay off as it may return again and again to a favorite perch.

- Be silent. If you are trying for digital photos, turn your camera on—but its sounds off.

In watching dragonflies, your best tools are your eyes, but sometimes they just don't see enough. Close-focus binoculars are a huge asset. (I use Eagle Optics Ranger 8x32 binoculars that focus to three feet, but there are many other fine choices.) Without needing to get super close, you should be able to make out the key features to identify your quarry. If you have an insect in hand, you can look through the opposite end of your binoculars to see highly magnified details.

Sometimes, even binoculars aren't enough. These insects are often quickly gone and you are left wondering about the width of the thoracic stripes, the color of the eyes, and the color of the wingtips. Capturing a photograph of the elusive creature leaves you with a lasting image that you can examine later at leisure.

If you have any kind of digital camera, you should be able to get reasonable photos to help with identification, even if you don't achieve masterpieces. Take lots of pictures in the hope that a few will show you features you want to see. One tactic is to take photos from the moment you see something new, and as you creep ever closer, keep snapping more photos. Never mind that you'll delete nine out of ten of them when you get home, at least you will have something other than "the one that got away."

In many species, an ideal situation asks for a top down photo, a photo of the front of the face, or a photo of the sides of the thorax. In my experience, this is wishful thinking: take what you can get!

Photographers use a variety of setups; some use single lens reflex cameras (SLRs, which have detachable lenses). I have a Fujifilm Finepix HS 30 EXR "bridge" camera, with a 30X zoom. To the pros, this is a mere toy, but it has the advantage of being lightweight and all-in-one (no fumbling to change lenses). And easy, if you use it without a tripod—a virtue if you are in the field, scrambling over rocks or pushing through underbrush.

The real key to getting striking photos is to make sure your whole subject is in focus and that the background is not fussy and distracting. Experiment with different focal depths (f-stops) to make your subject stand out from its surroundings. Aim for a background of blue sky, grey water, or solid green leaf rather than a tangle of tawny, dragonfly-colored vegetation.

Odonate Anatomy and Color Forms

Before trying to identify a dragonfly, it helps to know the commonly used terms for the body parts.

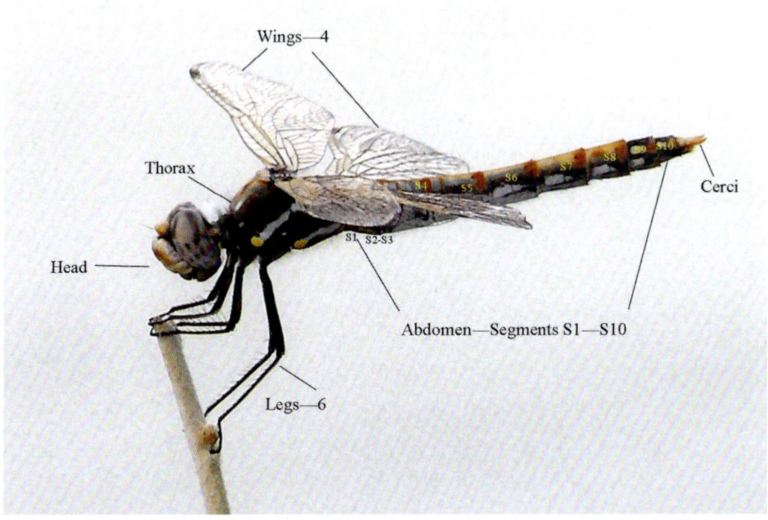

In many dragonfly species, males and females don't look alike and you might mistake them for different species. For this reason, it helps to establish whether you are looking at a male or a female.

Some damselfly species have two color forms of females. One is brightly colored and male-like and the other is very different—perhaps brown, or drab, or less conspicuous. The simplest way to tell which males and females belong together is to catch them "in the act." It is quite common to see pairs flying in tandem or in the wheel formation.

To add to the challenge, as dragonflies age their color may change. An individual's color may even vary in intensity at different temperatures, from dull-colored in the morning chill to bright in the midday heat.

How to use this book to identify your find

So, you see a UFO (that's Unidentified Flying Odonate)—what next? The key that follows gives brief notes on which features are helpful to note in each family. In general, focusing on the following features will help in identification:

- Color or stripes on the thorax
- Color or patterns on the abdomen
- Color and placement of the eyes
- Presence or absence of patterning in the wings
- Color and shape of the pterostigma (that's the colored tag on the leading edge of each wing towards the wing tip.)

Several behavioral features also help in narrowing down possibilities:
- Does the dragonfly fly constantly?
- Does the dragonfly perch?
- How are the wings held at rest?

The term "dragonfly" is commonly used as shorthand to refer to all members of the Odonate family of insects including the damselflies. When information applies only to damselflies that will be specified.

Use the key to determine first whether you have seen a dragonfly or a damselfly. Look for the family characteristics that best match your find. Then move to that section of the book.

Each species page gives information on habitat, appearance, size, flight season, behavior, and similar species. Size refers to total length of the dragonfly and is taken from Paulson (see Resources, page 99). Flight season (shown by green on the bar of months) comes from a Colorado database that records early and late dates for each species. They are approximate as this information continually changes as more is learned. Assume that photographs are of males, or of pairs, unless otherwise labeled.

SIMPLE KEY TO THE GROUPS

Dragonflies - large, chunky, strong fliers that perch with their unequally shaped wings out to the side, or slightly drooped forward; huge eyes meet, or almost meet, over the top of the head.

 Darners – large, fast fliers that rarely perch

 Clubtails – eyes spaced apart or barely meeting

 Emeralds (includes Baskettails) – often have green eyes (not so obvious in baskettails); fast, constant fliers

 Skimmers – includes most perchers and easy-to-see pond dragonflies

Damselflies - small, dainty, frail and weak fliers; wings folded over backs or loosely angled downwards by sides when perching; eyes are separated like those of hammerhead sharks.

 Broadwings – large, showy, wide wings, often metallic coloring

 Spreadwings – wings at 45°angle to side of body

Pond Damsels – small, with clear wings, shortish legs

 Bluets – wings usually lie closed along abdomen at rest

 Forktails – tiny, often with blue-tipped tails

 Dancers – "flirty" wings raised slightly above back

SPECIES ACCOUNTS
AND PHOTOGRAPHS

DRAGONFLIES (ANISOPTERA)

Dragonflies are large, chunky, typically strong fliers that perch with their unequally shaped wings out to the side, or very slightly drooped forward. They have huge eyes that meet, or almost meet, over the top of the head.

Darners
Family Aeshnidae

Darners are large, strong fliers with huge heads—mostly eyes—and skinny, darning-needle shaped abdomens. (I think of them as helicopter-like.) They spend most of the day in flight, and it's a great treat to find them perched.

Apart from the Common Green Darner, the rest of the darners seen in our area have similar rich, mosaic coloring, and can be a challenge to tell apart from one another.

Look for the presence and shape of colored top and side stripes on the thorax, and the shape and length of the abdominal appendages. Both these features are important in determining the species. Male darners usually have slender "waists."

Sedge Darner — *Aeshna juncea*

Habitat: Sedge beds around lakes, ponds, and fens. Montane and subalpine.

Appearance: Wide green to blue-green thoracic side stripes and obvious frontal stripes. **Male** has greenish eyes and thin black line across face. **Female** has two forms, one with blue eyes and body markings, the other with greenish eyes and greenish-yellow markings.

Total Length: 61 – 69 mm (2 3/8 – 2 3/4 inches)

Behavior: Flies, and frequently hovers, just above the tops of sedge beds in fairly short patrols along shorelines. Follows a regular and predictable flight path.

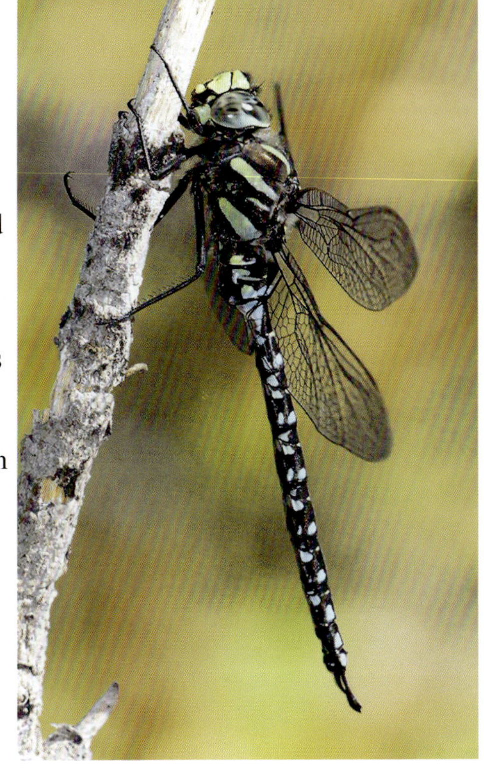

Look-alikes: Superficially appears like the Variable Darner, but with much wider thoracic stripes, and similar to the Paddle-tailed Darner (in flight), but with wider thoracic stripes and smaller abdominal appendages.

Other: The Sedge Darner is common around high country lakes with sedgy edges. The scientific name *juncea* means "of the rushes," referring to its usual habitat.

Mar	Apr	May	Jun	Jul	Aug	Sep	Oct	Nov

Lake Darner

Aeshna eremita

Habitat: Wooded lakes and large ponds. A northern and mountain species.

Appearance: Two side stripes on thorax, upper one notched, may have mark between them. **Male** has turquoise eyes, black line across face. **Female** has two forms, one blue like male, the other a mosaic of brown and greenish-yellow.

Total Length: 66 – 79 mm (2 5/8 – 3 1/8 inches)

Behavior: Cruises along lake shores often at knee to waist height; doesn't hover. Abdomen tip may droop downward and appear slightly J-shaped in flight. Females lay eggs into floating vegetation, floating logs or stumps of wood.

Look-alikes: None in this area.

Other: The Lake Darner is the largest of the so-called *mosaic* darners (genus *Aeshna*) that occur in our area.

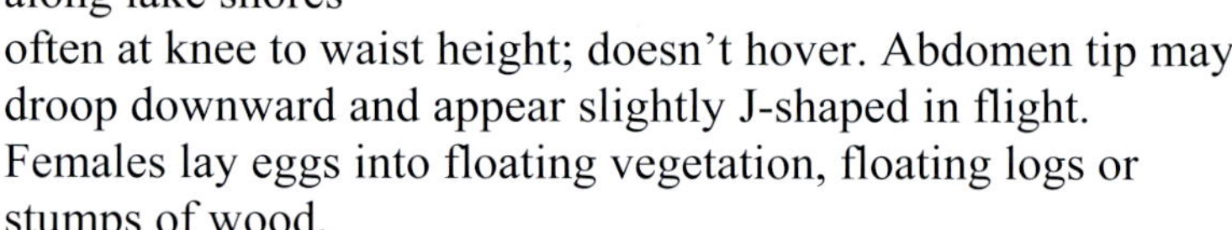

Mar	Apr	May	Jun	Jul	Aug	Sep	Oct	Nov

Variable Darner   *Aeshna interrupta*

Habitat: All sizes of vegetated ponds and lakes, from plains to mountains.

Appearance: Brown thorax with thin, often faint side stripes, often broken. The dorsal thoracic stripes may be present or absent. Abdomen dark with dorsal and lateral spots. **Male** has dull blue eyes, greenish face with thin, dark line. **Female** is like male, or more often yellow or greenish-yellow.

Total Length: 61 – 72 mm (2 3/8 – 2 7/8 inches)

Behavior: Flies along shorelines and in and out of sedge beds, often hovering. Feeds until late in the day. Females lay eggs in floating sedges, grasses, and upright stems or twigs.

Look-alikes: No other darners have such skinny thoracic stripes—often hard to see in flight. Paddle-tailed Darner is similar, but sturdier. Shadow Darner has smaller blue spots on the abdomen.

Other: Variable Darners are sometimes seen far from water in woodland clearings.

Mar	Apr	May	Jun	Jul	Aug	Sep	Oct	Nov

Paddle-tailed Darner   *Aeshna palmata*

Habitat: Lakes and ponds—however small—and slow streams.

Appearance: Thorax brown, with straight yellowish side stripes with a dot—or two—between them. Frontal stripe obvious, sometimes like an exclamation mark. **Male** (top) has blue-green eyes, black line across face, paddle-shaped abdominal appendages. **Female** is similar to male, or has brown, green and yellow mosaic patterns.

Total Length: 65 – 75 mm (2 1/2 – 3 inches)

Behavior: Flies knee to head high along shores and in and out of bays, hovering and poking into small clearings in emergent vegetation. Often hangs up vertically in brushy or grassy vegetation near the shore, providing a good opportunity for a photograph.

Look-alikes: Shadow darner lacks black face line, has narrower side stripes, and smaller blue spots.

Other: This is one of the most commonly seen blue darners in this area; it is second only to the Blue-eyed Darner.

Shadow Darner   *Aeshna umbrosa*

Habitat: Small streams, lakes and ponds. Foothills to mountains.

Appearance: Less blue, more brown than all other mosaic darners. **Male** has thin greenish-yellow dark-edged side stripes on thorax. Paddle-shaped abdominal appendages. **Female** is similar to male, or is drab and yellowish with brown eyes.

Total Length: 64 – 75 mm (2 1/2 – 3 inches)

Behavior: Plies up and down streams (or along pond banks), frequently hovering for many seconds. Hunts late in the day until dark; also hunts in the shade.

Look-alikes: Paddle-tailed Darners lack paired pale blue dots under the abdomen.

Other: "Mosaic" darners are tricky to tell apart unless you find them perched, or net them. Shadow Darners and Paddle-tailed Darners often occur together, making it even harder!

Mar	Apr	May	Jun	Jul	Aug	Sep	Oct	Nov

Blue-eyed Darner   *Rhionaeschna multicolor*

Habitat: Lakes, ponds, and slow streams.

Appearance: Male is a large, blue-and-brown-patterned darner with vivid blue eyes. Thorax brown with straight blue side stripes. **Female** comes in two forms: one is paler version of male; the other is less brightly colored with green-yellow and brown markings and greenish eyes.

Total Length: 65 – 69 mm (2 1/2 – 2 3/4 inches)

Behavior: Fast and direct flier. Often patrols at cattail-top level or in and out of bays around a shoreline. Occurs far from water, even over city streets, parks and yards.

Look-alikes: No other darner in our area has such bright blue eyes as this male. Paddle-tailed and Variable Darner females are similar to Blue-eyed Darner females in flight.

Other: Blue-eyed Darners are the most common mosaic darners seen in the area throughout the season.

Common Green Darner   *Anax junius*

Habitat: Ponds, marshes, lakes, and slow streams.

Appearance: "Bull's eye" mark on head. Unmarked bright green thorax. **Male** abdomen (right) is mostly blue with dark dorsal stripe. **Female** and **Immature** abdomen may be like male, or may be darkish red.

Total Length: 68 – 78 mm (2 5/8 – 3 1/8 inches)

Behavior: Fast flier that feeds over open area. Lays eggs, in tandem, into stems or floating vegetation. This species is more likely than other darners to perch in low vegetation.

Look-alikes: None in this area

Other: Common Green Darners are widespread and have a long flight season. Some of them are migratory and may first appear in early April. This species often congregates with other dragonflies in mixed feeding swarms far from the water.

Mar	Apr	May	Jun	Jul	Aug	Sep	Oct	Nov

Clubtails

Family Gomphidae

It is a real coup to find a clubtail, for they are rarely obvious and never numerous even in habitats that suit them. They tend to perch on rocks, bare ground, or in low vegetation, and they often fly just above the water surface as they patrol shorelines.

Clubtail is a good description of the male: the end of the abdomen is enlarged into a prominent bulge. The female has a hint of a club, but unlike the male, the club is not often obvious.

Look for the color and shape of the "club," the patterning along the sides of the abdomen, and the stripes on the sides of the thorax. This group is unusual among dragonflies in that the eyes are somewhat spaced and don't meet at a line on top of the head.

Sulphur-tipped Clubtail   *Gomphus militaris*

Habitat: Open ponds and lakes, and slow flowing rivers. Plains.

Appearance: Small clubtail with much yellow. **Male** has blue eyes on pale face. Thorax green and black. Dark, elongated pyramids pointing forward on each side of the abdomen and moderate-sized dull orange club.
Female is much like male, except lacks enlarged club.

Total Length: 47 – 53 mm (1 7/8 – 2 1/8 inches)

Behavior: Perches on sandy shores, dirt roads, and low vegetation and flies out for brief forays. Female found farther from the water than male.

Look-alikes: No similar species occur regularly in this area.

Other: Notice the huge eyes that do not meet at the mid line.

Mar	Apr	May	Jun	Jul	Aug	Sep	Oct	Nov

Pale Snaketail   *Ophiogomphus severus*

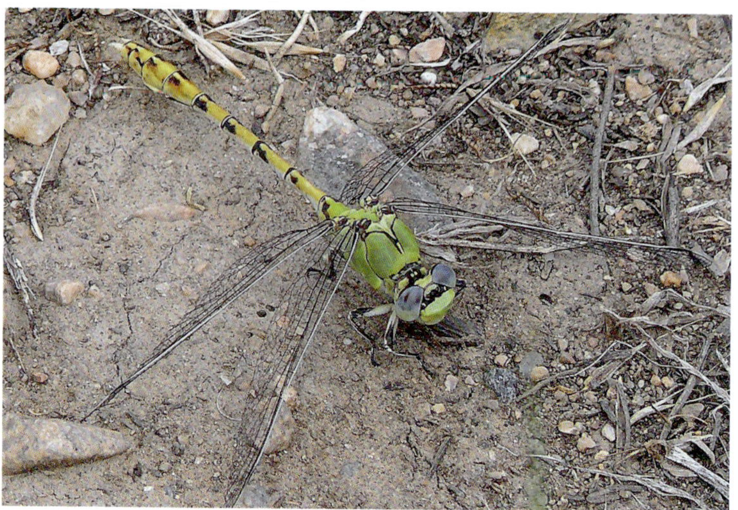

Habitat: Streams and small rivers with sandy or rocky banks, sandy lakes and gravel pits.

Appearance: Sexes somewhat similar. Striking blue, separated eyes and green face. Bright green, lightly marked thorax. Dull yellow abdomen with blotchy dark marks along the sides and white coloring below that shows more on the female.

Total Length: 49 – 52 mm (1 7/8 – 2 inches)

Behavior: Spends much time perched on sandy or gravelly banks, dirt roads, or streamside rocks, and takes brief flights to feed above riffles before returning to the same perch.

Look-alikes: None in this area. Female Pondhawks (bright green, also) can fool you for a moment, but snaketails' eyes do not meet in the middle of the head.

Other: These snaketails make good photographic subjects since they perch in the open and will stay put if you move slowly.

Mar	Apr	May	Jun	Jul	Aug	Sep	Oct	Nov

Emeralds
Family Corduliidae

Emeralds (including baskettails) are small to midsized dragonflies with relatively drab base coloring sometimes overlaid with a metallic sheen. Some have thoracic stripes, but they are not as prominent as you would see among the darners. They are elusive, fast fliers.

The emeralds are named for the eye coloring of mature individuals, which can often be quite stunning—like glowing green headlamps! But not all emeralds are this bright: the baskettails, which belong within this group, have duller eyes.

Look for the green eye color, the presence or absence of abdominal marking (some emeralds have white rings in the abdomen). Note the shape of the abdominal appendages (if you get that close!); it can be diagnostic.

American Emerald *Cordulia shurtleffii*

Habitat: Beaver ponds and boggy lakes, most often in forested areas. Mountains.

Appearance: Fuzzy brown thorax and black abdomen marked only by thin white line just below "waist." **Male** has greenish highlights on thorax, metallic green eyes, and the abdomen is slightly clubbed (not a pronounced club as in the clubtails). **Female** is stouter and lacks club.

Male is top left

Total Length: 43 – 50 mm (1 3/4 – 2 inches)

Behavior: Flies over lakes, ponds, and forest clearings in rapid forays, interrupted by brief hovering. Usually flies from knee to shoulder high, and may hang vertically on trees, or perch horizontally on vegetation.

Look-alikes: The rarer Ocellated Emerald (reported from only Larimer County) has more obvious green metallic thoracic spots.

Other: Shurtleff was a friend of the scientist who first described this species in the 1860s.

Mar	Apr	May	Jun	Jul	Aug	Sep	Oct	Nov

Hudsonian Emerald   *Somatochlora hudsonica*

Habitat: Boggy-edged lakes and ponds, and small streams. Mountains.

Appearance: Male has bright green eyes, metallic green thorax, and white-ringed abdomen. Distinctively shaped abdominal appendages. **Female** is similar in coloring to the male.

Total Length: 50 – 54 mm (2 – 2 1/8 inches)

Behavior: Flies just above the water around the shorelines of lakes and ponds, as it seeks food or a mate. Rarely comes to rest.

Look-alikes: None in this area.

Other: A male, found chilled but still living after a first cold night of fall, became a perfect study subject until it warmed up and flew again.

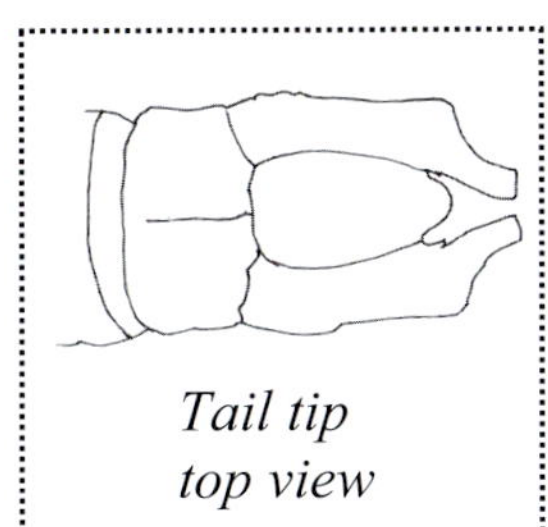

Tail tip
top view

Mar	Apr	May	Jun	Jul	Aug	Sep	Oct	Nov

Mountain Emerald *Somatochlora semicircularis*

Habitat: Sedge meadows and small ponds. Mountains.

Appearance: Furry-looking bronze or greenish thorax with yellowish marks on sides that become masked with age. **Female** is much like male.

Total Length: 47 – 52 mm (1 7/8 – 2 inches)

Behavior: Forages over sedge meadows and woodland clearings; may fly from knee-high to treetop level. Rests between forays, often hanging vertically from twigs.

Look-alikes: Hudsonian Emerald has abdominal rings; American Emerald male has a slight club.

Other: Paulson (see Resources, page 99) notes that "dragonfly graveyards" of this species have been seen with many bodies floating on the pond surface after reaching the natural end of their lives.

Mar	Apr	May	Jun	Jul	Aug	Sep	Oct	Nov

Dot-winged Baskettail   *Epitheca petechialis*

Habitat: Ponds, lakes, slow streams and irrigation ditches.

Appearance: Dark body. Face yellowish, green eyes develop with age. Thorax has yellow side dots. Abdomen has dull orange marks along sides. Wings have variable dark blotches near base and (usually) dark veins along leading edge of inner wing. Female is like male, but has duller eyes.

Total Length: 43 – 47 mm (1 3/4 – 1 7/8 inches)

Behavior: Persistent flier and hoverer, with unpredictable fast flight. Patrols fairly low along shore lines, up and down small streams, and in clearings or woodland edges.

Look-alikes: Similar to the Common Baskettail, which is not known in this area.

Other: Be aware! Newly hatched dragonflies may hold their wings folded above their backs, contradicting the mantra that dragonflies have "wings out to the side."

Mar	Apr	May	Jun	Jul	Aug	Sep	Oct	Nov

Skimmers

Family Libellulidae

The skimmers comprise our largest dragonfly group. They are showy and noticeable and come in many forms. Members of this diverse group have large eyes that touch at the top of the head, and "boot shaped" hind wing cells called the anal loop.

Look for wing color and pattern, if present. Some skimmers have dots or dashes at various angles on the abdomen, while others have plain-colored abdomens. Fresh colors may be dulled by a powdery or waxy white or pale blue coating, called pruinescence.

As this family is large, it helps to become familiar with the different genera within it:

- Whitetails - white abdomens (not tails)
- King Skimmers - or just Skimmers (genus *Libellula*)
- Amberwings - small and wasp-like
- Pennants - wings like flags
- Whitefaces - males have gleaming white faces
- Pondhawks - predatory and low perching
- Meadowhawks - often red, late season, in meadows
- Dashers - quick out and back, and often "obelisk" in the sun
- Saddlebags - the wing markings look like panniers
- Gliders - nearly always airborne

Desert Whitetail   *Plathemis subornata*

Habitat: Ponds and slow streams. Plains (and desert).

Appearance: Male has dramatic black and white wing patterns, with white along the trailing edges of the wings nearest the body. Faint yellow side marks on thorax. White, pruinose (waxy coated) abdomen. **Female** has zigzag dark wing markings, no white. Yellow thoracic stripes and parallel dotted lines on abdomen. **Immature** resembles female.

Total Length: 40 – 51 mm (1 5/8 – 2 inches)

Behavior: Similar to Common Whitetail. Perches on the ground, or low in vegetation.

Look-alikes: Common Whitetail male has less white on wings. Widow Skimmer male (in mourning) has "black near his heart." Eight-spotted Skimmer female has fewer black wing patches and they are not zigzag.

Other: Desert Whitetails are more common to the east and south of the state, but have also been recorded from Larimer and Denver counties.

Mar	Apr	May	Jun	Jul	Aug	Sep	Oct	Nov

Common Whitetail
Plathemis lydia

Habitat: Muddy-bottomed ponds and lakeshores, even cattle wallows and puddles.

Appearance: Male has striking, unmistakable wing pattern. Abdomen pale blue to white with pruinose (waxy) coating. **Immature male** has male-like wing patches and female-like abdomen. **Female** has brown thorax with whitish-yellow side stripes. Abdomen brown with yellow diagonal side slashes. Wings have smaller, but more numerous dark patches.

Total Length: 42 – 48 mm (1 5/8 – 1 7/8 inches)

Behavior: Perches on ground or low on twigs or snags. Males are aggressive to other males, chasing them off. Female lays eggs in shallows, bobbing and dipping repeatedly in the same area, while male often guards from above.

Look-alikes: The Desert Whitetail male has more white on the wings. The female Twelve-spotted Skimmer has parallel (not diagonal) yellow slashes along the abdomen.

Other: Common Whitetails are often found alongside Widow Skimmers, but they may show up at the ponds slightly later in the day.

Mar	Apr	May	Jun	Jul	Aug	Sep	Oct	Nov

Four-spotted Skimmer

Libellula quadrimaculata

Habitat: Lakes, ponds, acidic bogs, and slow streams. A northern and often high elevation species.

Appearance: Dark pterostigmata and dark nodes (mid points along leading edge of wing) make up the four spots per pair of wings. Hind wings have dark, angled patches at base. Overall color is brown to red-brown marked with yellow on the sides of the somewhat flattened abdomen. Color dulls with age.

Total Length: 42 – 46 mm (1 5/8 – 1 3/4 inches)

Behavior: Territorial. Males aggressively chase other males. Perches on reeds, vegetation, or ground. Can be the most numerous skimmer seen at some boggy, acidic ponds.

Look-alikes: None

Other: This northern and circumpolar species is Alaska's state insect.

Mar	Apr	May	Jun	Jul	Aug	Sep	Oct	Nov

Flame Skimmer *Libellula saturata*

Habitat: Ponds, lakes and slow streams.

Appearance: Male has vivid orange body, prominent orange wing patches, and orange face. **Female** has orange-brown thorax and abdomen with faint light line on upper thorax. Wings less vivid than male, with most color along leading edges.

Total Length: 52 – 61 mm (2 – 2 3/8 inches)

Behavior: Alternates patrolling with perching on stream or lake bank vegetation. Male may defend a territory, but the area may vary from day to day. Female flicks water droplets and eggs forward as she flies above the water surface. Some eggs drop into the water, while others fall on the moist shore.

Look-alikes: None in this area.

Other: This eye-catching, and aptly named, skimmer is primarily southern and western, but seems to be moving into the Front Range from the south.

Mar	Apr	May	Jun	Jul	Aug	Sep	Oct	Nov

Eight-spotted Skimmer   *Libellula forensis*

Habitat: Lakes and ponds.

Appearance: Male has dark and white patches alternating on wings (there's a total of eight black spots on all wings combined). Thorax brown with yellow side stripes. Abdomen pruinose (waxy-coated). **Female** thorax is like male. Wings may or not have white. Abdomen has parallel yellow dashes on the upper sides.

Total Length: 49 – 51 mm (1 7/8 – 2 inches)

Behavior: Alternates hunting with long periods perching; defends no fixed territory.

Look-alikes: Similar to Twelve-spotted Skimmer, but fewer wing patches. Female Common Whitetail has slanted yellow slashes on abdomen, not parallel rows.

Other: Where Twelve-spotted and Eight-spotted Skimmers fly together, check the males' spots closest to the wingtips: black = twelve, white = eight.

| Mar | Apr | May | Jun | Jul | Aug | Sep | Oct | Nov |

Twelve-spotted Skimmer   *Libellula pulchella*

Habitat: Vegetated lakes and ponds, irrigation ditches.

Appearance: Male has alternating black and white wing patches (a total of twelve dark spots altogether on the wings), two pale thoracic side stripes, and pruinose (white, waxy-coated) abdomen in age. **Female** lacks the white wing patches, but has the same six black patches per wing pair as the male, and parallel yellow dashes down sides of abdomen.

Total Length: 53 – 57 mm (2 1/8 – 2 1/4 inches)

Behavior: Conspicuous flights over ponds, punctuated by perching, often on favorite twigs or emergent cattails. Aggressive to other males of same (and other) species.

Look-alikes: Eight-spotted Skimmer lacks black near the wing-tips. Common Whitetail female has angled, not lined up, yellow dashes on the abdomen.

Other: This widespread species lives in all 48 contiguous states and in southern Canada.

Mar	Apr	May	Jun	Jul	Aug	Sep	Oct	Nov

Widow Skimmer

Libellula luctuosa

Habitat: Lakes, ponds, and stream backwaters; farm ponds.

Appearance: Male has eye-catching black and white wing patches that fill two-thirds of the wings, with "black next to the heart." Pruinose (waxy coated and whitish) front thorax and abdomen. **Female** shows tan spots on lateral thorax. Yellow line on upper thorax split into two along abdomen. Wingtips are sometimes dark.

Total Length: 38 – 40 mm (1 1/2 – 1 5/8 inches)

Behavior: Male flies short patrols along margins of ponds and lakes, sending off intruding males. Perches frequently, and returns to a favorite lookout time and time again. Immatures lurk low in tall grasses and other vegetation, as do females until they're ready to copulate or lay eggs.

Look-alikes: None

Other: Striking and ever present, this is often the dragonfly species that people first consciously notice.

Mar	Apr	May	Jun	Jul	Aug	Sep	Oct	Nov

Roseate Skimmer　　　*Orthemis ferruginea*

Habitat: Ponds, ditches and open marshes with muddy bottoms.

Appearance: Male has red-lilac thorax and pink-red abdomen. Eyes dark red. **Female** has brown thorax with patterns, abdomen reddish-brown. Face dull brown or tan.

Total Length: 48 – 53 mm (1 7/8 – 2 1/8 inches)

Behavior: Males are territorial and patrol pond and stream edges. Both sexes are perchers and often select twigs or weeds quite close to the ground.

Look-alikes: None

Other: Though southern in origin, this eye-catching skimmer has recently been found in Larimer County. Males are so striking that any range expansion is likely to be noticed.

Mar	Apr	May	Jun	Jul	Aug	Sep	Oct	Nov

Eastern Amberwing   *Perithemis tenera*

Habitat: Muddy-bottomed ponds, lake shores and slow streams. Plains.

Appearance: Tiny skimmer with wasp-like markings. **Male** has amber wings with yellow-bordered orange pterostigmata. Abdomen brownish-orange with lighter colored rings. **Female** has smudgy dark wing patches—usually less completely colored than male.

Total Length: 20 – 25 mm (3/4 – 1 inch)

Behavior: Male perches just above water on emergent twigs. Pairs flit just above algal mats, which comprise small territories that the male defends. Males will send off other males, and will fly at look-alike wasps until they leave the area.

Look-alikes: None in this area

Other: Small and seemingly vulnerable, these dragonflies may derive protection by looking like wasps, thus deflecting predation.

Mar	Apr	May	Jun	Jul	Aug	Sep	Oct	Nov

Calico Pennant   *Celithemis elisa*

This immature male is yellow, as are females.

Habitat: Vegetated ponds and lakes and adjacent meadows.

Appearance: Male has distinctive wing patterns that include dark wingtips, dark node-spots, and large rusty-red hind wing patches. Pterostigmata orange-red. Black abdomen ornamented with row of red hearts. **Female** is more yellowish overall, including hind wing patches, pterostigmata, and heart shapes on dorsal abdomen.

Total Length: 29 – 34 mm (1 1/8 – 1 3/8 inches)

Behavior: Male perches on the tops of weedy vegetation, maintaining position even in breezy conditions—hence the name pennant? Female is more likely to stay hidden in long grass until she is ready to mate. Showy and dainty in flight.

Look-alikes: None

Other: This mainly eastern species was found in Colorado in 2002, at Pella Crossing near Hygiene in Boulder County.

Mar	Apr	May	Jun	Jul	Aug	Sep	Oct	Nov

Halloween Pennant   *Celithemis eponina*

Habitat: Lakes, marshes and ponds with edge vegetation.

Appearance: Male has broad, dark wing patches on a pale orange background and orange pterostigmata (Halloween colors). Red markings on dorsal abdomen. **Female** has yellower wings and yellower thoracic side stripes than male.

Total Length: 36 – 42 mm (1 3/8 – 1 5/8 inches)

Behavior: Perches on twigs and weed tips, wings held high and "pennant-like;" flight is butterfly-like. Pairs stay in "wheel" for several minutes, and then fly out over open water for egg-laying—often still paired.

Look-alikes: None in this area.

Other: At the height of their flight season, you can see these dragonflies perched on tall plants every yard or so along a pond bank, often swaying in the breeze.

Mar	Apr	May	Jun	Jul	Aug	Sep	Oct	Nov

Belted Whiteface   *Leucorrhinia proxima*

Habitat: Boggy, vegetated ponds especially in forested areas of the foothills, montane, and subalpine zones.

Appearance: Male's dark thorax and first two segments of abdomen are splashed with crimson. Face gleaming white. **Female** has red markings like male or similarly-placed dull yellow markings.

Total Length: 33 – 36 mm (1 1/4 – 1 3/8 inches)

Behavior: Male defends small territory and perches among emergent vegetation to await female. Mating pairs, perched in reed beds or on shrub tangles on the bank, stay in wheel for many minutes.

Look-alikes: Crimson-ringed Whiteface (male and female) are similar, but much less likely to be encountered; told apart by details of wing veins.

Other: The Belted Whiteface (called the Red-waisted Whiteface in older publications) is a widespread northern and high elevation species.

Mar	Apr	May	Jun	Jul	Aug	Sep	Oct	Nov

Dot-tailed Whiteface *Leucorrhinia intacta*

Habitat: Small, open ponds and lakes with emergent plants.

Appearance: Male is a small, black dragonfly with white face and creamy-yellow or white dot on the dorsal abdomen S7 (see the diagram on page 13). **Female** is browner than male with yellowish markings on lateral abdomen that darken with age, and yellow S7 spot. **Immature** is similar to female.

Total Length: 29 – 33 mm (1 1/8 – 1 1/4 inches)

Behavior: Ground or low-vegetation percher, often selecting pale-colored roads or gravel on which to bask. On the water, the male defends a small territory around his chosen lookout.

Look-alikes: The Black Meadowhawk lacks a white face and white tail spot. Other female whitefaces resemble this one, but the shape and size of the yellow tail dot is diagnostic.

Other: Many plains ponds have large numbers of this species early in the flight season.

Mar	Apr	May	Jun	Jul	Aug	Sep	Oct	Nov

Hudsonian Whiteface   *Leucorrhinia hudsonica*

Habitat: Sedge meadows and boggy ponds in woodland clearings. Mountains.

Appearance: Male has white face; thorax red with a black triangle on top and black markings on the sides. Abdomen prominently marked with red on top. **Female** may be male-like, or may have yellow where the male has red.

Total Length: 27 – 32 mm (1 1/8 – 1 1/4 inches)

Behavior: Male defends a tiny territory, perching on sedges or grasses. Female is more often seen perched on the ground or on low snags, in clearings away from water.

Look-alikes: The Boreal Whiteface, with similar red coloring, is larger.

Other: The flight period of this species coincides with an abundance of mosquito prey.

Mar	Apr	May	Jun	Jul	Aug	Sep	Oct	Nov

Crimson-ringed Whiteface

Leucorrhinia glacialis

Habitat: Boggy or marshy ponds, usually in forested areas of the mountains.

Appearance: Male has dark thorax and abdomen, marked with bright red—the "ring" in the name refers to the red near the "waist" at S1-2 (see diagram on page 13). Bright white face. **Female** may be like male, or may have yellow where male has red.

Total Length: 34 – 35 mm (1 3/8 inches)

Behavior: Perches on ground, or flat on vegetation, or in trees. Undergoes a long copulation away from the water.

Look-alikes: Belted Whiteface is virtually identical at a glance, and only an examination of wing venation in hand can tell these species apart.

Other: At this point, only a few records of this mostly northern species have been documented in Colorado, from Boulder and Larimer counties. The flight season (below) is based on these few records.

Mar	Apr	May	Jun	Jul	Aug	Sep	Oct	Nov

Boreal Whiteface   *Leucorrhinia borealis*

Habitat: Marshy ponds and bogs with emergent rushes and reeds. Mountains.

Appearance: Male has dark brown eyes and white face, red-brown and black-patterned thorax, red-spotted black abdomen. **Female** may be like duller version of male or may have yellow where the male shows red.

Total Length: 44 – 46 mm (1 3/4 inches)

Behavior: Perches on the ground or on emergent vegetation over the water. These whitefaces can be abundant in the right habitat and don't seem to be aggressively territorial.

Look-alikes: The Hudsonian Whiteface is smaller. Female Boreal Whitefaces are like Belted and Crimson-ringed Whiteface females except for the larger size and the pale spot on S7 (see page 13).

Other: As you might guess from the name "boreal," this is primarily a northern species known from Alaska, Canada and northern Minnesota. There are a few records from Larimer County.

Mar	Apr	May	Jun	Jul	Aug	Sep	Oct	Nov

Eastern Pondhawk   *Erythemis simplicicollis*

Habitat: Any well-vegetated pond, lakeshore, marsh, ditch, or slow stream.

Appearance: Male has blue-green eyes and green face, pruinose (waxy-coated) blue thorax and abdomen, and white abdominal appendages. Color varies with age. **Female's** thorax and first part of the abdomen is bright green, the rest of the abdomen is patterned in black and pale green or white. **Immature** is similar to female.

Total Length: 38 – 44 mm (1 1/2 – 1 3/4 in)

Behavior: Perches on the ground, on mats of vegetation, and on low vegetation. Fierce predator of other dragonflies and damselflies. Females and immatures often are seen in bank vegetation or meadows far away from the water. Able to thrive in less-than-pristine ponds.

Look-alikes: Western Pondhawk male has black abdominal appendages. Female Western Pondhawk has less obviously patterned green abdomen, with dark dorsal line. Blue Dasher has striped thorax and often perches with wings drooped forward.

Other: Eastern and Western Pondhawks both occur at the same ponds at roughly the same season, and they may hybridize (or be effectively a single species?) .

Mar	Apr	May	Jun	Jul	Aug	Sep	Oct	Nov

Western Pondhawk — *Erythemis collocata*

Habitat: Slow or still waters of ponds, lakeshores, marshes and ditches.

Appearance: Medium-sized skimmer. **Male** has pruinose (powder blue and waxy) color, green face. Abdominal appendages dark. **Female** is green, with a black line on the dorsal surface. Her abdominal appendages are pale. **Immature** resembles female in coloring.

Total Length: 40 – 42 mm (1 5/8 inches)

Behavior: Males tend to perch on the ground, on fallen logs in the water, or on mats of floating vegetation, returning to the same perch after short forays. Females are more often seen lurking low among grass or other vegetation and are more skittish than males.

Look-alikes: Eastern Pondhawk male has white abdominal appendages; female abdomen is banded in black and white. Male Blue Dasher has stripes on thorax and often perches with wings drooped forward.

Other: Eastern and Western Pondhawks both occur at the same ponds at roughly the same season, and they may hybridize (or be effectively a single species?).

Mar	Apr	May	Jun	Jul	Aug	Sep	Oct	Nov

Variegated Meadowhawk
Sympetrum corruptum

Habitat: Shallow ponds, lakes, marshes and slow streams.

Appearance: Male has thorax with white-yellow stripes or spots on side. Abdomen intricately patterned in brown and red with lateral "portholes" of creamy white. Female (and immature) is yellower than male. Leading edge wing veins golden. Legs black and yellow.

Total Length: 39 – 42 mm (1 1/2 - 1 5/8 inches)

Behavior: Makes short forays over the pond to feed, and perches on twigs, stems, or trees in between flights. This meadowhawk has a long flight season, and in colder periods will warm up by basking on gravel roads or sun-warmed rocks.

Look-alikes: None. No other meadowhawk has such an elaborate (variegated) pattern.

Other: A migratory species, this dragonfly may be the first dragonfly to be seen in spring. Variegated Meadowhawks that emerge locally will not appear until the ponds have warmed. It's not known how—or if—the migratory and the hatch-here populations are interconnected.

| Mar | Apr | May | Jun | Jul | Aug | Sep | Oct | Nov |

Red-veined Meadowhawk
Sympetrum madidum

Habitat: Shallow, vegetated ponds and marshes—even those drying in late season.

Appearance: Male is predominantly red, including wing bases and leading-edge veins of wings. Black legs. A hint of dark marks along sides of abdomen. **Female** is straw-colored to (sometimes) red. Abdomen with dark marks on sides of S4-7 (see page 13), and whitish below.

Total Length: 42 – 45 mm (1 5/8 – 1 3/4 inches)

Behavior: Perches in low vegetation, or on gravel roadsides or rocks to warm up. Female lays eggs in shallows, with male either in tandem, or guarding her from above.

Look-alikes: Female Striped Meadowhawks have similar thoracic stripes, but lack the reddish tinge at base of wings.

Other: Primarily a northwestern species, this dragonfly recently has been sighted in the Front Range, suggesting either it is expanding its reach, or it has been here and unrecognized.

Mar	Apr	May	Jun	Jul	Aug	Sep	Oct	Nov

White-faced Meadowhawk
Sympetrum obtrusum

Habitat: Shallow ponds, bogs and marshes, sedge beds.

Appearance: Male has brown eyes and gleaming white face. Thorax brown. Abdomen red with black triangles along the lower sides. Black legs. **Female's** eyes are brown over green, the face is yellowish. Thorax brown, but with pale sides. Abdomen tan with line of dark marks on lower sides.

Total Length: 31 – 39 mm (1 1/4 - 1 1/2 inches)

Behavior: Perches in low vegetation, makes short forays to feed or to hook up with female. Not aggressively territorial (many can be seen together in right habitat).

Look-alikes: Cherry-faced Meadowhawk has similar black-on-red abdomen, but face is never bright white. Female Striped Meadowhawk (and immature male) has more distinct stripes on thorax, not just a pale patch.

Other: I've seen a vividly colored male in very late season warm up by basking flat on a silvery tree stump by an almost dry seasonal pond.

Mar	Apr	May	Jun	Jul	Aug	Sep	Oct	Nov

Striped Meadowhawk   *Sympetrum pallipes*

Habitat: Shallow ponds and marshes, and floodplains.

Appearance: Male thorax is brown with creamy-yellow side and dorsal stripes. Abdomen red with varying amounts of black. Eyes brown and face tan. **Female** is similar to male, but paler, with brown and pale green eyes.

Total Length: 34 – 38 mm (1 3/8 – 1 1/2 inches)

Behavior: Perches in sedges and rushes, or on bank snags. It is common to see many pairs close together, or many females laying eggs in the same general area.

Look-alikes: No other adult meadowhawk has thoracic stripes like this, although some immature meadowhawks, including Variegated Meadowhawks, can show striping.

Other: Although the Latin name means "pale footed," this is not a reliable characteristic for identification.

Mar	Apr	May	Jun	Jul	Aug	Sep	Oct	Nov

Cherry-faced Meadowhawk
Sympetrum internum

Habitat: Ponds, lakes and ephemeral wet meadows bordering them. Montane zone.

Appearance: Male has red-brown thorax and red abdomen with black adjoining half-circles or triangles along sides. Eyes are brown, the face reddish, not always cherry red. **Female** is marked as male, but duller tan, becoming redder with age.

Total Length: 31 – 36 mm (1 1/4 – 1 3/8 inches)

Behavior: Perches and feeds in the low vegetation of flooded pond margins and wet meadows. Females, alone or in tandem, drop eggs over shallows and wet meadows and even above grass that might flood the following spring.

Look-alikes: The White-faced Meadowhawk male lacks the cherry-red face.

Other: Although often the most abundant red meadowhawk seen in the montane, its numbers may drop in extended periods of drought.

Mar	Apr	May	Jun	Jul	Aug	Sep	Oct	Nov

Saffron-winged Meadowhawk
Sympetrum costiferum

Habitat: Ponds, lakes and marshes, even alkaline areas. Plains, foothills, montane.

Appearance: Male's thorax is red-brown. Abdomen dull red, sometimes with low, lateral black markings. Leading-edge wing veins golden to orange and pterostigmata red. Legs brown. **Female** is less red than male, with black-framed yellow pterostigmata. Legs brown.

Total Length: 31 – 37 mm (1 1/4 – 1 1/2 inches)

Behavior: Paulson (see Resources, page 99)

describes the egg laying as "in tandem . . . in open water but also on wet shore"—and very methodical.

Look-alikes: Autumn Meadowhawk lacks the golden leading-edge wing veins. Cherry-faced Meadowhawk and White-faced Meadowhawk have black legs. Female Autumn Meadowhawk has noticeable "sore-thumb" protrusion beneath the abdomen tip.

Other: DuBois (see Resources, page 99) notes that this species has been seen above 11,000 feet in Gunnison County, Colorado. In parts of its range, this species is known to fly into late fall; however, the flight season in Colorado is not yet well known.

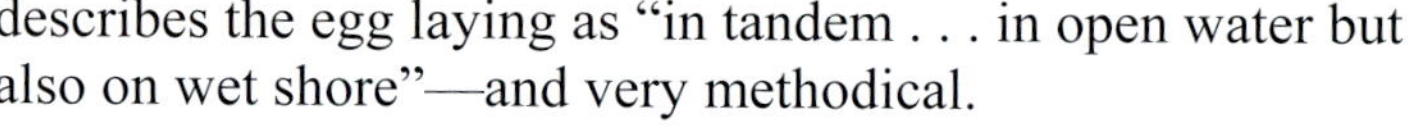

Mar	Apr	May	Jun	Jul	Aug	Sep	Oct	Nov

Band-winged Meadowhawk
Sympetrum semicinctum

Habitat: Ponds, marshes, seeps and meadows.

Appearance: Male's thorax is red-brown with narrow dark lines from the legs to the wing bases. Abdomen red with black lateral stripes. **Female** is duller and yellowish tan. Both sexes have orange-amber wing patches extending the width of the wings and darker towards the wing nodes.

Total Length: 28 – 40 mm (1 1/8 – 1 5/8 inches)

Behavior: Perches on fences, shrubs, and tall twigs (such as yucca stalks) sometimes far from water.

Look-alikes: No other meadowhawks have such distinctive, banded wings.

Other: In previous field guides, this species was known as the "Western Meadowhawk."

Black Meadowhawk *Sympetrum danae*

Habitat: Sedge marshes and shallow, sedge-lined shorelines of ponds and lakes.

Appearance: Male is dark brown to black when mature. Younger males may still show yellowish, female-like marking. **Female** has tan face and reddish-brown over pale green eyes. Thorax has eye-catching yellow patterning on brown base. Abdomen has black lateral stripe, and is whitish below.

Total Length: 30 – 33 mm (1 1/8 – 1 1/4 inches)

Behavior: Males perch low in sedges, or in brushy marginal vegetation. Females stay back from the water until ready to mate. Eggs laid in tandem, often in the shallows of reed beds.

Look-alikes: Male is all black and quite unlike other species in the area. Female has striping on the thorax like Band-winged Meadowhawk, but has clear wings.

Other: This species can thrive at high elevation, and DuBois (see Resources, page 99) notes, "overwintering eggs have been recorded to survive for nine weeks in a block of ice."

Mar	Apr	May	Jun	Jul	Aug	Sep	Oct	Nov

Autumn Meadowhawk *Sympetrum vicinum*

Habitat: Ponds or lakes with surrounding woodland.

Appearance: Male (right) has brown eyes and fuzzy brown thorax. Abdomen red with slight dark mark on dorsal tip (S9). Legs red-brown. **Female** (left) has tan thorax and tan to dull red abdomen. Legs pale. Prominent stubby subgenital plate sticks out like a sore thumb on the ventral surface of the abdomen tip.

Total Length: 31 – 35 mm (1 1/4 - 1 3/8 inches)

Behavior: Late season flier that spends time basking on gravel roads, boardwalks, and sheltered shrubs. Eggs may be laid in shallow water or in wet vegetation.

Look-alikes: Saffron-winged Meadowhawk males are larger and darker red. Autumn meadowhawk female appearance is unique in the region.

Other: Appropriately enough, this is one of the last meadowhawks to fly in the fall. Autumn Meadowhawks can even survive moderate frosts.

Mar	Apr	May	Jun	Jul	Aug	Sep	Oct	Nov

Blue Dasher   *Pachydiplax longipennis*

Habitat: Weedy ponds, lakes and slow streams with plentiful vegetation.

Appearance: Male has striped thorax, teal-green eyes, and white face dark at the top (some people think it looks puppy-like.) Wings often have a tinge of yellow. Abdomens of older males become dull blue with a pruinose (waxy) coating. **Female** has distinct yellow dashes on a dark background along the abdomen.

Total Length: 28 – 45 mm (1 1/8 – 1 3/4 inches)

Behavior: Often perches with wings drooped forward. Points abdomen upwards in obelisk position when it's hot and sunny, to reduce the sun's heating effect on its body.

Look-alikes: Pondhawk males somewhat resemble Blue Dashers, but pondhawks do not have thoracic stripes. They also tend to be ground perchers, whereas Blue Dashers cling to twigs or stems.

Other: Males defend breeding territories, even sending off much larger, but superficially look-alike, male pondhawks.

Mar	Apr	May	Jun	Jul	Aug	Sep	Oct	Nov

Red Saddlebags   *Tramea onusta*

Habitat: Lakes, ponds, irrigation ditches, farm ponds and slow pools in streams.

Appearance: Male has red eye-tops and face. Large, velvety red patch on hind wings, thus inspiring the common name. Red and black abdomen. **Female** is duller overall, with tan wing patches and abdomen.

Total Length: 41 – 49 mm (1 5/8 – 1 7/8 inches)

Behavior: A strong flier, this dragonfly spends much time on the wing and rarely perches. It may be seen far from water and may be a part of large, mixed feeding swarms.

Look-alikes: None, if you get a good look at the wing colors.

Other: Although not common here, this species is known to migrate, and is known to join mixed swarms, so it could well be more widespread than our records suggest.

Mar	Apr	May	Jun	Jul	Aug	Sep	Oct	Nov

Black Saddlebags   *Tramea lacerata*

Habitat: Shallow ponds and lakes with surrounding vegetation.

Appearance: Male and **Female** are similar. Both are strong fliers that seem heavy and hunched in flight, because of the large, black patch on each hind wing (saddlebags). Eyes and face dark. Abdomen black. **Immatures** may have pale marks on the upper surface (males on S7, females on several segments).

Total Length: 51 – 55 mm (2 – 2 1/8 inches)

Behavior: Most often seen in flight. Adults patrol just above the pond or lake surface, alone or in tandem pairs. Males are territorial and chase off other males. Fall adults migrate south, often in mixed swarms with darners, gliders, and meadowhawks.

Look-alikes: Red Saddlebags has red velvety hind wing patches that can look dark in poor light.

Other: These dragonflies, with their distinctive flight profile, can be recognized easily when they form part of feeding swarms, and when they migrate.

Mar	Apr	May	Jun	Jul	Aug	Sep	Oct	Nov

Wandering Glider　　　*Pantala flavescens*

Habitat: Small, and often temporary, bodies of standing water in open areas.

Appearance: Usually seen in flight. Gives overall impression of being yellow-orange or even golden—and fast. Wings are clear, hind wings are large.

Total Length: 47 – 50 mm (1 7/8 – 2 inches)

Behavior: Feeds at head height over meadows, often patrolling a fixed beat. Strong fliers, these dragonflies are known to migrate over impressively long distances. This is a global species. Mixed swarms of dragonflies often include Wandering Gliders.

Look-alikes: The Spot-winged Glider is the same shape, but looks browner in flight and with a distinct dot on each hind wing near the body.

 Other: The Wandering Glider has been tracked migrating from India to Africa, aided by strong tail winds—a long-distance record?

Mar	Apr	May	Jun	Jul	Aug	Sep	Oct	Nov

Spot-winged Glider   *Pantala hymenaea*

Habitat: Small, and often temporary, bodies of standing water in open areas.

Appearance: Most often seen in flight, and has an overall brown to brownish-red color. Eyes and face reddish in color. Dots on the hind wings near the body are diagnostic, but not always easy to see in flight.

Total Length: 45 – 50 mm (1 3/4 - 2 inches)

Behavior: These gliders behave like Wandering Gliders and may form part of mixed swarms. These fliers generally perch only at night. They have been seen in Boulder and Larimer counties, but tend to be more common farther east in the state.

Look-alikes: The Wandering Glider is golden-yellow and has no wing spots.

 Other: The Spot-winged Glider and Wandering Glider are the only two species in this genus. Although not distributed globally like the Wandering Glider, Spot-winged Gliders are found across North America and as far south as Chile.

Mar	Apr	May	Jun	Jul	Aug	Sep	Oct	Nov

SPECIES ACCOUNTS AND PHOTOGRAPHS

DAMSELFLIES (ZYGOPTERA)

Damselflies are small, dainty, and usually frail and weak fliers. They hold their similar-shaped wings folded over their backs or loosely angled downwards by their sides. The eyes are well separated like those of hammerhead sharks.

Broadwings
Family Calopterygidae

This family is characterized by wings that are broader (relative to their length) in comparison to spreadwings or pond damselflies. They hold their wings obliquely above the abdomen. The wings are variously colored.

In our area, there is only one representative of the family so identification is straightforward.

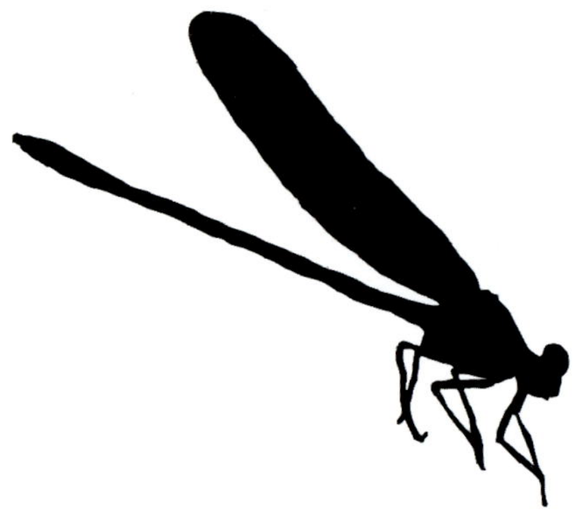

American Rubyspot   *Hetaerina americana*

Habitat: Streams and irrigations ditches, sometimes straying to nearby ponds.

Appearance: Large damselfly with flashy red wing bases and often metallic body coloration. Wings fairly wide and, at rest, held at an angle above the back. **Female** is duller colored, with stockier abdomen.

Total Length: 38 – 46 mm (1 1/2 - 1 3/4 inches)

Behavior: Territorial. Will defend a stretch of river bank against other males. Often perches and returns again and again to the same grass stem or twig only a few inches to knee high above the water. May roost in groups at night.

Look-alikes: None in this area.

Other: A related species, the River Jewelwing (*Calopteryx aequabilis*) is known in the northern Front Range from only a couple of historic records and hasn't been seen recently.

Mar	Apr	May	Jun	Jul	Aug	Sep	Oct	Nov

Spreadwings
Family Lestidae

Spreadwings have a characteristic way of perching with their wings held at roughly a 45° angle out to the side. (Some teneral (just emerged) pond damsels may do this to some extent, so beware.) These damsels are medium to large. They tend to hang at an angle in vegetation, not flat on a surface. Their wings appear relatively short in comparison with the length of the abdomen, partly because of the wing position at rest.

Look for wing position and perching angle at rest. The wings also seem to be "stalked" in that they are narrow near the body. Some spreadwings have metallic coloring when fresh. More commonly, spreadwings have pale coloration, sometimes pruinose (waxy-coated) in age.

Great Spreadwing   *Archilestes grandis*

Habitat: Ponds and slow streams, often with ample tree cover.

Appearance: Large, robust spreadwing. **Male** has vivid blue eyes. Pale, yellowish stripe on each side of the thorax. **Female's** eyes are blue to brown. Thorax markings like male. Abdomen sturdy with noticeably enlarged tip.

Total Length: 50 – 62 mm (2 – 2 1/2 inches)

Behavior: Rests and roosts hanging at a downward angle, or almost vertically, and looks like a pale, gauzy arrow. Female lays her eggs—either solo or clasped by her male—inside stems or twigs, sometimes high above the water.

Look-alikes: None in this area.

Other: Although there have been spring sightings, these large spreadwings are far more common in late season. These damsels often perch on the far side of stems and seem to watch you intently with one eye at each side of the stem.

Mar	Apr	May	Jun	Jul	Aug	Sep	Oct	Nov

Spotted Spreadwing *Lestes congener*

Habitat: Ponds and lakes with emergent vegetation.

Appearance: Drab, brownish spreadwing with clear wings. **Male** and **Female** similar except for the male's somewhat blue eyes. Thorax is bicolored, with the upper part dark (with a faint tan line) and the lower part white with two prominent dark spots at the lower edge (look carefully).

Total Length: 31 – 42 mm (1 1/4 – 1 5/8 inches)

Behavior: Can be seen in great numbers at suitable locations, with many pairs ovipositing in the stems of rushes and cattails. Overwinter as eggs, withstanding very low temperatures. Hatch in late spring.

Look-alikes: Northern Spreadwing is superficially like the Spotted Spreadwing, especially when both are pruinose (have a waxy coating that obscures the base coloring). Northern Spreadwing lacks the two spots on the side of the thorax.

Other: A tandem pair, chilled and barely mobile, was found by a pond at 8,000 feet elevation in the first week of October.

Mar	Apr	May	Jun	Jul	Aug	Sep	Oct	Nov

Northern and Southern Spreadwings
Lestes disjunctus and Lestes australis

Northern Spreadwing male

Northern and Southern Spreadwings used to be considered one species, but they are different enough in the hands of an expert to qualify as separate species. Southern Spreadwings tend to be found on the eastern plains, the Northern Spreadwings occur more to the west.

Habitat: Ponds and lakes with ample vegetation and often boggy edges.

Appearance: Medium-sized spreadwing looks dark when its colors are fresh. Thorax with pale, slim midline and wider bluish side stripe. Later, male colors become overlaid by pruinosity (waxy coating) that renders everything dullish blue. **Female** is dark above and stouter looking.

Total Length:
    Northern Spreadwing 33 – 42 mm (1 1/4 – 1 5/8 inches)
    Southern Spreadwing 36 – 46 mm (1 3/8 – 1 3/4 inches)

Continued next page

Behavior: Adults stay away from water until sexually mature. Then you may see clouds of these mid-sized spreadwings hovering among, and just above, the sedge beds at the edge of ponds and lakes. Females lay egg clusters inside sedge stalks.

Look-alikes: Lyre-tipped Spreadwing, especially the female. The pale patch on the back of the female's head reaches the eyes on the Lyre-tipped Spreadwing, but stops before the eyes on the Northern Spreadwing. Lyre-tipped males have "claspers" that are distinctive and look like lyres. Southern Spreadwings are very similar to Northern Spreadwings, but the Southern is slightly longer (36 – 46 mm). Where the two species both occur, they can be separated from one another only in hand.

Other: The female slices vertical sedge stalks with her ovipositor, and then deposits eggs in the incisions.

Mar	Apr	May	Jun	Jul	Aug	Sep	Oct	Nov

Northern Spreadwing

Mar	Apr	May	Jun	Jul	Aug	Sep	Oct	Nov

Southern Spreadwing

Lyre-tipped Spreadwing

Lestes unguiculatus

Habitat: Shallow marshes and marshy pond and lake edges, often areas that quickly dry.

Appearance: Looks like Northern Spreadwing at first glance. Lyre-shaped claspers of **male** are diagnostic (if you get a close enough look). **Both sexes** have wing pterostigmata with light-colored ends. Back of the **female's** head is pale up to near the eyes, with more white than the Northern Spreadwing.

Total Length: 31 – 44 mm (1 1/4 – 1 3/4 inches)

Behavior: Often found in areas subject to drying out. Female lays eggs over dry ground a short distance from the water. This species is quick to colonize newly flooded areas. May be especially common in prairie potholes.

Look-alikes: Northern Spreadwing has less white on the back of the head, and its pterostigmata are single colored.

Other: The lyre in "lyre-tipped" refers to the shape of the musical instrument of that name.

| Mar | Apr | May | Jun | Jul | Aug | Sep | Oct | Nov |

Emerald Spreadwing *Lestes dryas*

Habitat: Small ephemeral ponds, often in woodlands. Often seen in the montane to alpine zones.

Appearance: Bright, sturdy spreadwing with brilliant metallic green or bluish-green coloring. Female has noticeably large ovipositor and is altogether chunkier than the male.

Total Length: 32 – 40 mm (1 1/4 - 1 5/8 inches)

Behavior: Female lays large eggs, singly, into stems of sedges, rushes, and even willow leaves. Eggs may overwinter, and

then hatch in spring when ponds enlarge with melt water. They develop fast—to beat the drying of their ponds.

Look-alikes: No other spreadwings have the same emerald brilliance.

Other: This species seems to breed best in ponds lacking predators such as fish or the larvae of large dragonflies.

Mar	Apr	May	Jun	Jul	Aug	Sep	Oct	Nov

Pond Damsels
Family Coenagrionidae

Pond Damsels lurk around plants, gleaning insects like reef fish gleaning food from coral. They are frail, weak fliers and rarely fly far. Many are hard to identify, except in hand.

- **Bluets** hold their wings along the abdomen when they are at rest.

Look for the balance of blue and black on the abdomen, the color of the final three segments, and the side stripes on the thorax. Note the size and shape of eyespots (behind the eyes).

- **Forktails** are tiny. Males tend to be brightly colored at both ends and darker in the middle. Females may come in a male-like form, or be so different in color you might think them another species.

  Look for dots on the upper thorax, colors on the thorax sides, and color on the tail tip including where it begins and ends.

- **Dancers** are often blue and black, and can be confused with bluets. At rest, they hold their wings above (not quite parallel to) the abdomen. In flight, they are flirty and butterfly-like.

  Look for the shape of the thoracic side stripes and if those stripes are forked, the shape and color of the abdominal patterns, and the extent of the tail-tip color.

- **Red Damsels** are represented by a single species in this area, and thus present no identification challenge.

Taiga Bluet

Coenagrion resolutum

Habitat: Sedge marshes and fens, sedge-dense edges of upland lakes and ponds.

Appearance: Male is blue, or blue green, and black, with more black on the hind end of the abdomen than other commonly seen bluets. Has distinct "U" shape in black on the upper surface of the second abdominal segment (S2). Female can be of two forms— mostly brown, or mostly green.

Total Length: 27 – 33 mm (1 1/8 – 1 1/4 inches)

Behavior: These tiny bluets are northern and high elevation species (up to over 11,000 feet). Males and females usually meet and mate away from the pond, hovering in and around low woody vegetation. They stay together as the female lays eggs into below-surface vegetation.

Look-alikes: The Boreal Bluet is larger, has less black on the abdomen, and lacks the "U."

Other: This is the only representative of the Eurasian Bluets *(Coenagrion)* found in our area. In general, the Eurasian bluets are very similar to the American bluets but it is not clear if the groups are closely related.

Mar	Apr	May	Jun	Jul	Aug	Sep	Oct	Nov

Arroyo Bluet   *Enallagma praevarum*

Habitat: Ponds and slow streams with ample vegetation.

Appearance: Male has mostly blue thorax with thin black side stripe. Abdomen more black than blue in mid segments, with noticeable blue rings. Abdominal segments S8-9 all blue. Large blue eyespots at the rear of the eyes are joined by a blue bar making them dumb-bell shaped. **Female** has two forms, one male-like but paler than male in its blue areas, the other brown and black.

Total Length: 26 – 35 mm (1 – 1 3/8 inches)

Behavior: Males are easier to find than females when you scan the water's edge, unless you spot mating pairs. Females lay eggs into underwater plant material.

Similar Species: Male Tule Bluet is larger and has less black on the middle segments. Female Tule, Familiar, and River Bluets are all larger than this species—but tricky to identify.

Other: This damselfly, a common southern species, often inhabits desert arroyos, hence its common name.

Mar	Apr	May	Jun	Jul	Aug	Sep	Oct	Nov

River Bluet *Enallagma anna*

Habitat: Small to midsized streams and irrigation ditches with gentle to moderate flow.

Appearance: Male is typical blue and black bluet, with much black on S6-7. From above, black areas point toward the front. Long, narrow abdominal appendages. **Female** may be blue form or brown form; both have narrow black thoracic shoulder stripes.

Total Length: 30 – 36 mm (1 1/8 – 1 3/8 inches)

Behavior: The female may lay eggs in tandem, or solo, and goes underwater to do so; she may stay down for half an hour. Larvae overwinter in late developmental stage, so they are ready to emerge in late spring.

Look-alikes: Tule Bluet and Arroyo Bluet males have similar mix of black and blue, but they are both smaller than the River Bluet. Females are harder to tell apart from females of other bluet species except in the hand.

Other: The males have long abdominal appendages that may be visible with close-focus binoculars. Even so, this species is difficult to identify except in the hand.

Mar	Apr	May	Jun	Jul	Aug	Sep	Oct	Nov

Flight Season not well known

Familiar Bluet   *Enallagma civile*

Habitat: Lakes, ponds, marshes with emergent vegetation.
Widespread.

Appearance: Male is a bluet with more blue than black. Blue
eyespots on back of eyes. Abdomen mostly blue on segments
S2-5, and mostly black on S6-7. Tail tip (S8-9) all blue.
Female may be like a pale male or be overall brown and tan.

Total Length: 28 – 39 mm (1 1/8 – 1 1/2 inches)

Behavior: Gleans food from the surface of vegetation, picking
at prey like a fish picks at a coral reef. Mating pairs, and also
tandem pairs laying eggs, can be numerous in good habitat.

Look-alikes: Several bluet males are like this one (including
Boreal and Northern Bluets), but generally have more black on
the abdomen. Females of this, and other, bluet species can be
told apart only in hand.

Other: Scores of exuviae (hatch cases) found on wooden
uprights of a fishing dock suggest mass emergence of this
species—probably a strategy to maximize survival during
predation.

Mar	Apr	May	Jun	Jul	Aug	Sep	Oct	Nov

Tule Bluet   *Enallagma carunculatum*

Habitat: Lakes, ponds, cattail marshes and farm ponds.

Appearance: Male is blue and black. Eyes are blue capped in black. Abdominal segments S3-6 more than half black, and S7 almost completely black. Tail tip (S8-9) all blue. **Female** may be male-like blue form or brown form. Like many other bluet females, best matched with male counterparts by seeing tandem pairs.

Total Length: 26 – 37 mm (1 – 1 1/2 inches)

Behavior: Typical of bluets, feeds and rests in low, pond-side vegetation and adjacent meadows, gleaning prey by delicate picking.

Look-alikes: Boreal, Familiar, and Northern Bluet males have less black on middle segments. Females are similar to many other bluet females, and can be told apart only in hand.

Other: Accurate identification of bluets, especially female bluets, often requires close-up investigation.

 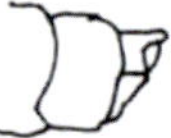 *Male Tule (L) and Familiar (R) Bluet tail tips from side*

Mar	Apr	May	Jun	Jul	Aug	Sep	Oct	Nov

Alkali Bluet   *Enallagma clausum*

Habitat: Alkaline and saline ponds, lake shores.

Appearance: Male has blue and black thorax with fairly narrow black side stripe. Abdomen has more black on segments approaching the tip, but S8-9 is blue. Large blue dumbbell eye spots. **Female** may be blue male-like form, or brown with tan or greenish eyes.

Total Length: 28 – 37 mm (1 1/8 – 1 1/2 inches)

Behavior: May be present in large numbers in the right alkaline habitat, and in some lakes may be the only bluets present. Female lays eggs into floating mats of algae, either on or just beneath the surface.

Similar Species: River Bluet has similar coloring—but usually different habitat. Arroyo and Tule Bluets have more black, and Familiar, Northern and Boreal Bluets have less black. Females can be told apart only by examining anatomical details in the hand.

Other: DuBois (see Guides, page 99) notes that larvae may crawl up to 50 feet from the water before settling on a place from which to emerge.

Mar	Apr	May	Jun	Jul	Aug	Sep	Oct	Nov

Northern Bluet and Boreal Bluet
Enallagma annexum and Enallagma boreale

These two species are so similar, except in hand, that they are often just called "Nobos." As with many bluets in our region, naming species can be highly technical. If you have reached that level of interest you have progressed beyond this book!

Habitat: Vegetated still water habitats.

Appearance: Blue and black typical bluets. **Males** of both species have blue tails

Northern Bluet male

(S8-9), mostly black on S6-7, and blue increasing on the low-number abdominal segments. Both species have two forms of females, blue (like male) or brown.

Total Length: 29 – 40 mm (1 1/8 – 1 5/8 inches); the Boreal Bluet is slightly smaller.

Behavior: These two species are also similar in behavior. They glean food from vegetation, perch low in bank or emergent plants, lay eggs in vegetation mats at the water surface or below with the males guarding.

Continued next page

Similar Species: Besides being like each other, these species could be confused with Familiar Bluets, which have only slightly more blue on a couple of the abdominal segments. This creates a challenge!

Other: Northern and Boreal males can be told apart by checking their abdominal appendages with magnification. They become slightly easier to determine only after you have been able to compare the two many times!

Mating wheel of Boreal Bluets

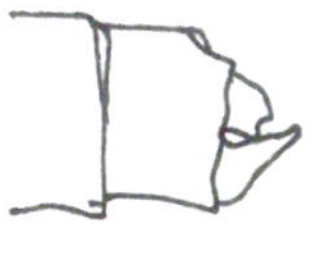

Northern Bluet tail tip

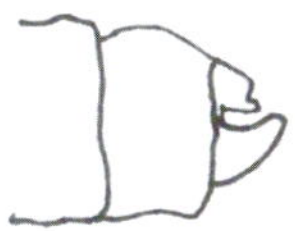

Boreal Bluet tail tip

Northern Bluet flight season

Mar	Apr	May	Jun	Jul	Aug	Sep	Oct	Nov

Boreal Bluet flight season

Mar	Apr	May	Jun	Jul	Aug	Sep	Oct	Nov

Rainbow Bluet *Enallagma antennatum*

Habitat: Well-vegetated slow streams and rivers, also ponds.

Appearance: Male's common name says it all—rainbow: face is orange, thorax greenish, abdomen blue, and legs yellow. **Female** is yellowish-green, with brown eyes.

Total Length: 27 – 33 mm (1 1/8 – 1 1/4 inches)

Behavior: Pairs stay together as the female lays eggs in emergent grasses at the edge of the pond or river. She may completely submerge during the process—and he may help haul her out again.

Look-alikes: None, although you might mistake this for a forktail at first glance.

Other: An eastern plains species, this dainty bluet is quite common in a few locations, but never abundant in this area.

Mar	Apr	May	Jun	Jul	Aug	Sep	Oct	Nov

Double-striped Bluet   *Enallagma basidens*

Habitat: Lakes, ponds and slow stream with emergent vegetation.

Appearance: Minute, common blue and black bluet, unmistakable if you look for the double stripe on the side of the thorax (really a dark shoulder stripe divided by a light band along most of its length) of both **male** and **female**.

Total Length: 21 – 28 mm (7/8 – 1 1/8 inches)

Behavior: These tiny, delicate-seeming bluets can be the most common damsels around ponds at times, with males and male-female wheels perched or flying above the ponds in small clouds.

Look-alikes: None

Other: This tiny wisp of bluet-hood seems to be expanding its range—or was it overlooked before because of its minute size?

Mar	Apr	May	Jun	Jul	Aug	Sep	Oct	Nov

Orange Bluet *Enallagma signatum*

Habitat: Lakes, ponds, gravel pits and small streams.

Appearance: Slender. **Male** is bright orange and black with orange eyes. **Female** is like a paler version of male, or greenish blue.

Total Length: 28 – 37 mm (1 1/8 – 1 1/2 inches)

Behavior: Most common later in the day, according to Paulson (see Resources, page 99). Perches in shrubs or trees, or in sedge or grass beds. Lays eggs in tandem, and female (or both sexes) may submerge while the eggs are injected into vegetation or algal mats.

Look-alikes: None in this area.

Other: Relatively few have been seen in this area, but this book includes the species because, as bluets go, it's relatively easy to identify with its orange body and eyes!

Mar	Apr	May	Jun	Jul	Aug	Sep	Oct	Nov

Pacific Forktail and Plains Forktail
Ischnura cervula and Ischnura damula

Plains Forktail male

These two species are very similar and both may be found in our area. The Plains Forktail is common and well documented east of the Continental Divide; the Pacific Forktail is less often recorded in the Front Range.

Habitat: Edges of lakes, ponds, marshes and ditches.

Appearance: Male has black thorax, blue at the sides, with four blue dots on dorsal surface. Abdomen is black except S8-9 vivid blue, resembling a tail light. **Female** may be like male, but not as bright, with four thoracic dots, or may be bluish or greenish (Plains), or orangey-pink or blue (Pacific) and lack thoracic dots.

Total Length:

Pacific Forktail 24 – 31 mm (1 – 1 1/4 inches)

Plains Forktail 23 – 34 mm (7/8 – 1 3/8 inches)

Continued next page

Plains Forktail female

Behavior: Appears to float in and among tall edge vegetation, sometimes in small clouds—males and females together. Lays eggs inside floating pond plants. Rarely ventures far from banks.

Look-alikes: Each other.

Other: A look at the male abdominal appendages is necessary to tell apart these species where they both occur. The Pacific Forktail has a larger "fork" sticking up from the dorsal tip of the abdomen.

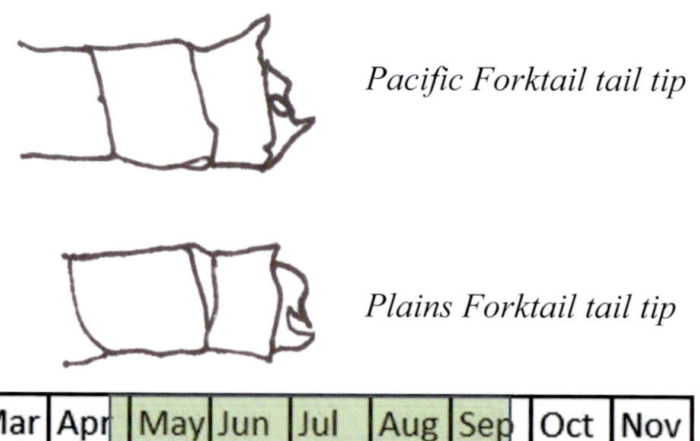

Pacific Forktail tail tip

Plains Forktail tail tip

Mar	Apr	May	Jun	Jul	Aug	Sep	Oct	Nov

Western Forktail
Ischnura perparva

Habitat: Sedge and grass beds and marshy pond and lake banks.

Appearance: Male has greenish eyes and face. Bright green thorax with wide black top and side stripes. Abdomen dark with a blue tip. **Female** has several forms—one male-like, one having orange-red thorax with black striping, another having an overall dull blue caste.

Total Length: 23 – 30 mm (7/8 – 1 1/8 inches)

Behavior: Small numbers of males and many more females lurk in dense vegetation. Females lay eggs, solo, into floating mats of plant material.

Similar Species: Eastern Forktail, except in the hand.

Other: Despite the geographical designation, both the western and eastern species (see next page) occur in parts of the Front Range. The name *perparva* means very small.

Mar	Apr	May	Jun	Jul	Aug	Sep	Oct	Nov

Eastern Forktail   *Ischnura verticalis*

Habitat: Marshy ponds and lakes with sedges and grasses.

Appearance: Male has greenish eyes and face. Bright green thorax with wide black top and side stripes. Blue-tipped dark abdomen. **Female** has thoracic stripes like the male, but the base color is orange. Females often become overall bluish or light gray in age, with a waxy coating.

Total Length: 20 – 33 mm (3/4 - 1 1/4 inches)

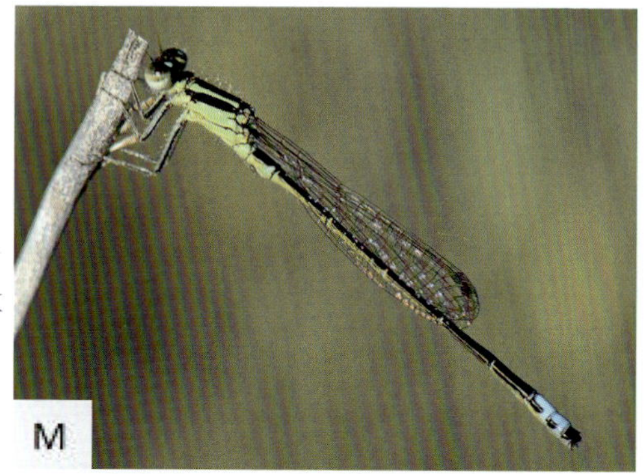

Behavior: Eastern and western forktails behave similarly. The females may flutter their wings at males, but not as a come on: it is a sign they are not receptive. Males are less likely to be out-numbered by females than in the case of Western Forktails (see Resources, Paulson, page 99).

Similar Species: Western Forktail, except in the hand.

Other: Both Eastern and Western Forktails are tiny and delicate looking, but surprisingly robust.

Mar	Apr	May	Jun	Jul	Aug	Sep	Oct	Nov

Western Red Damsel
Amphiagrion abbreviatum

Habitat: Marshes and seeps, sedge and grass beds bordering ponds.

Appearance: Male thorax may be red, reddish-brown, or black. Abdomen is dull red with black markings towards the tip. **Female** is variable from dull brown, to tan, to orange-red and chunkier than male.

Total Length: 24 – 28 mm (1 – 1 1/8 inches)

Behavior: Stays low in grasses and sedges, flitting from place to place inconspicuously, easily overlooked.

Look-alikes: This is the only red and black damsel in our area; it has no look-alikes.

Other: The Western Red Damsel is the only member of its genus to occur in Colorado. Early season is the best time to look for these tiny, unobtrusive damsels.

Mar	Apr	May	Jun	Jul	Aug	Sep	Oct	Nov

Blue-fronted Dancer *Argia apicalis*

Habitat: Muddy bottomed ponds, lakes, and gently flowing streams.

Appearance: Male has thorax of unpatterned blue with only a hint of a thin black shoulder stripe. Abdomen black above and tan at the sides, with blue tail tip (S8-10). **Female** is blue, like male, but with blue extending part way below the abdomen, or entirely brown, some with pale lines between abdominal segments.

Total Length: 33 – 40 mm (1 1/4 – 1 5/8 inches)

Behavior: Often a ground percher. Males arrive at the water first, and await females.

Look-alikes: None in this area

Other: Many dancers, this one among them, have bouncy, almost flirty, flight patterns.

Mar	Apr	May	Jun	Jul	Aug	Sep	Oct	Nov

Paiute Dancer   *Argia alberta*

Habitat: Shallow sedge marshes near springs, and the small streams that flow from them.

Appearance: Male has blue thorax with a black median stripe and forked side stripes. Abdomen has black on blue with the appearance of blue rings between segments, and blue segments 8-10. Wings are black-veined. **Female** has two forms. First form is male-like with blue thorax with forked stripe, and pale blue and black abdomen. Second form is overall tan and black. Both forms lack blue tail tip.

Total Length: 27 – 32 mm (1 1/8 – 1 1/4 inches)

Behavior: Perches on snags or low sedges. Couples are more prevalent in the afternoon. They lay eggs in tandem.

Look-alikes: Males could be confused with male bluets, except for their forked thoracic stripes and their raised wings at rest.

Other: This species also inhabits areas around hot springs.

Mar	Apr	May	Jun	Jul	Aug	Sep	Oct	Nov

Variable Dancer   *Argia fumipennis*

Habitat: Wide variety of sites from small ponds to vegetated irrigation channels and streams.

Appearance: Male has overall violet coloring. Abdomen has dark rings and narrow side markings. Tail tip is blue with a violet overlay on S8. **Female** has similar markings, but is overall brownish.

Total Length: 29 – 34 mm (1 1/8 – 1 3/8 inches)

Behavior: Males rest on snags or rocks near the water and are seen more often than females. In dancer fashion, these damsels slowly open and close their wings when at rest.

Look-alikes: Nothing similar occurs in our area

Other: The Variable Dancer is an eastern species that seems to be spreading westward into Colorado's plains counties. Some individuals have smoky wings.

Mar	Apr	May	Jun	Jul	Aug	Sep	Oct	Nov

Vivid Dancer   *Argia vivida*

Habitat: Small to medium shallow, slowly flowing streams and irrigation channels.

Appearance: Male has blue eyes. Thorax is electric blue with black median stripe and thin black side stripes. Abdomen is blue with round to triangular dorso-lateral black markings. **Female** may be all brown, or all blue, or a mixture of the two, with blue thorax and brown abdomen. Abdomen has black markings like male, regardless of base color.

Total Length: 29 – 38 mm (1 1/8 – 1 1/2 inches)

Behavior: Perches on rocks or vegetation close to the water. Injects eggs into underwater stems. Roosts in trees.

Look-alikes: No other male dancer in this area has such bright blue coloration. The female Springwater Dancer, which occurs farther south, resembles the female.

Other: We know of a population in the lower foothills that occupies a small area of gravelly trail and beaten-down weeds near a meager muddy and sluggish seep with watercress growing in it. So far, there have been individuals here for the last six years, reliably.

Emma's Dancer — *Argia emma*

Habitat: Clear streams and rivers, and sometimes lakes.

Appearance: Male has violet eyes. Thorax has light purple base color, fine dorsal and lateral stripes, and whitish underside. Abdomen is black on lilac, with blue tail tip. **Female** is overall light tan or olive green on thorax and first several abdominal segments. Eyes are brown.

Total Length: 33 – 40 mm (1 1/4 - 1 5/8 inches)

Behavior: Perches on bare ground or rocks. Lays eggs in tandem, in underwater vegetation including floating roots of willow.

Look-alikes: Variable Dancer has similar violet hue, but the tail tip is bicolored blue-lilac, not only blue.

Other: Emma's Dancer and the Vivid Dancer are probably the most common dancers in northern Colorado.

Mar	Apr	May	Jun	Jul	Aug	Sep	Oct	Nov

RESOURCES

Guides

Abbott, John C. 2005. *Dragonflies and Damselflies of Texas and the South-Central United States*. Princeton University Press, Princeton, New Jersey. (NOT field-guide sized!)

------. 2011. *Damselflies of Texas: A Field Guide*. Texas Natural History Guides. University of Texas Press, Austin. (Also available as an e-book.)

Biggs, Kathy. 2004. *Common Dragonflies of the Southwest: A Beginner's Pocket Guide*. Azalea Creek Publishing, Sebastopol, California. (Also available as an e-book under the title *Dragonflies of California and the Greater Southwest*.)

DuBois, Robert. 2012. *Dragonflies & Damselflies of the Rocky Mountains*. American Naturalist Series. Kollath+Stensaas Publishing, Duluth, Minnesota.

Nikula, Blair, Jackie Sones, Donald Stokes and Lillian Stokes. 2002. *Stokes Beginner's Guide to Dragonflies and Damselflies*. Little Brown and Company, New York.

Paulson, Dennis. 2009. *Dragonflies and Damselflies of the West*. Princeton Field Guides. Princeton University Press, Princeton, New Jersey. (Also available as an e-book.)

Groups and Internet Sites

Boulder County Audubon Society

www.boulderaudubon.org/dragonflies.htm

Photographs and brief descriptions of the most common dragonflies of Boulder County. This guide was compiled by Scott Severs, with support from Ann Cooper and Steve Jones.

Colorado Dragonfly Network

www.facebook.com/codragonflynetwork

An informal network of people interested in dragonflies and damselflies, this page is "for sharing enthusiasm, observations and photographs of dragonflies and damselflies in Colorado."

http://groups.yahoo.com/group/co_odes/

This chat group has a purpose similar to the one above, but attracts a slightly different group of users, so the conversations are not the same. It welcomes members of all levels of expertise. Topics include "discussion on ID, favorite places to see Odes, photography tips, books, conservation," and other topics.

Dragonfly Society of the Americas and Odonata Central

www.odonatacentral.org

Odonata Central hosts the official web site of the Dragonfly Society of the Americas. This site is a good source of checklists for various counties within the state that you might be exploring, and photos to help in identifying your find. You can also submit well-documented entries (collections or diagnostic photographs) of species you have seen.

Migratory Dragonfly Partnership

www.migratorydragonflypartnership.org

The Migratory Dragonfly Partnership, a collaboration between governmental, academic, and conservation groups coordinated by the Xerces Society for Invertebrate Conservation, aims "to better understand and conserve North America's dragonfly migration." As a citizen scientist, you can take part in this research.

Western Odonata

www.facebook.com/groups/WesternOdonata

This regional chat group on Facebook is an open group where dragonfly and damselfly enthusiasts can share observations, post photographs, and ask questions. Its focus is on western North America, and it is a lively forum.

GLOSSARY

Abdomen: Third, and hindmost, body part of an insect

Abdominal segments: Numbered segments from S1-S10 (starting at the "waist"), which sometimes have distinct coloration

Antenna (antennae): Sensory organs on the head of an insect

Cercus (cerci): Upper terminal appendage(s) of the male, or only prominent terminal appendage(s) of the female

Clasper: Informal term for appendage at the abdomen tip used by male to grasp the female during mating

Compound Eye: Large eye made of many (up to 30,000) individual visual units

Dorsal: Back or upper side (opposite is ventral)

Exoskeleton: Outer skeleton or shell

Exuvia (exuviae): Discarded larval shell(s)

Head: First, and front, body segment of an insect

Hemolymph: Plasma-like bug blood

Larva (larvae): Pre-adult form of an insect (also nymph or naiad)

Metamorphosis: Process of transformation from larval to adult form

Molt: Shedding of a larval shell (exuvia) to allow for growth

Node: Shallow notch on roughly the midpoint of the each wing's leading edge

Nymph: See larva

Obelisk: Body posture (tail stuck skyward) that reduces the

Glossary — continued

Ovipositor: Appendage located beneath the abdomen tip used by female for laying eggs

Pruinose: Having a white, waxy or powdery coating on the body surface

Pterostigma (pterostigmata): Thickened, often colored cell on the leading edge of an odonate wing near the tip

Spiracle: Small hole in the exoskeleton through which an adult odonate breathes

Tandem: Twosome posture where the male clasps the back of a female's head

Teneral: Just hatched adult stage in which the new exoskeleton is not yet hardened

Thorax: Second, or middle, body segment of an insect from which legs and wings originate

Ventral: Underside or belly (opposite of dorsal)

Wheel: Position during mating in which a male clasps a female by the back of the head while she swings her tail tip to reach the male's abdominal segment two and grabs his previously transferred sperm

CHECKLIST
Dragonflies and Damselflies of the Colorado Front Range

DRAGONFLIES

DARNERS

__Sedge Darner	*Aeshna juncea*
__Lake Darner	*Aeshna eremita*
__Variable Darner	*Aeshna interrupta*
__Paddle-tailed Darner	*Aeshna palmata*
__Shadow Darner	*Aeshna umbrosa*
__Blue-eyed Darner	*Rhionaeschna multicolor*
__Common Green Darner	*Anax junius*

CLUBTAILS

__Sulphur-tipped Clubtail	*Gomphus militaris*
__Pale Snaketail	*Ophiogomphus severus*

EMERALDS

__American Emerald	*Cordulia shurtleffii*
__Hudsonian Emerald	*Somatochlora hudsonica*
__Mountain Emerald	*Somatochlora semicircularis*
__Dot-winged Baskettail	*Epitheca petechialis*

SKIMMERS

__Desert Whitetail	*Plathemis subornata*
__Common Whitetail	*Plathemis lydia*
__Four-spotted Skimmer	*Libellula quadrimaculata*
__Flame Skimmer	*Libellula saturata*
__Eight-spotted Skimmer	*Libellula forensis*
__Twelve-spotted Skimmer	*Libellula pulchella*

__Widow Skimmer — *Libellula luctuosa*

__Roseate Skimmer — *Orthemis ferruginea*

__Eastern Amberwing — *Perithemis tenera*

__Calico Pennant — *Celithemis elisa*

__Halloween Pennant — *Celithemis eponina*

__Belted Whiteface — *Leucorrhinia proxima*

__Dot-tailed Whiteface — *Leucorrhinia intacta*

__Hudsonian Whiteface — *Leucorrhinia hudsonica*

__Crimson-ringed Whiteface — *Leucorrhinia glacialis*

__Boreal Whiteface — *Leucorrhinia borealis*

__Eastern Pondhawk — *Erythemis simplicicollis*

__Western Pondhawk — *Erythemis collocata*

__Variegated Meadowhawk — *Sympetrum corruptum*

__Red-veined Meadowhawk — *Sympetrum madidum*

__White-faced Meadowhawk — *Sympetrum obtrusum*

__Striped Meadowhawk — *Sympetrum pallipes*

__Cherry-faced Meadowhawk — *Sympetrum internum*

__Saffron-winged Meadowhawk — *Sympetrum costiferum*

__Band-winged Meadowhawk — *Sympetrum semicinctum*

__Black Meadowhawk — *Sympetrum danae*

__Autumn Meadowhawk — *Sympetrum vicinum*

__Blue Dasher — *Pachydiplax longipennis*

__Red Saddlebags — *Tramea onusta*

__Black Saddlebags — *Tramea lacerata*

__Wandering Glider — *Pantala flavescens*

__Spot-winged Glider — *Pantala hymenaea*

DAMSELFLIES

RUBYSPOT
__American Rubyspot   *Hetaerina americana*

SPREADWINGS
__Great Spreadwing   *Archilestes grandis*
__Spotted Spreadwing   *Lestes congener*
__Northern Spreadwing   *Lestes disjunctus*
__Southern Spreadwing   *Lestes australis*
__Lyre-tipped Spreadwing   *Lestes unguiculatus*
__Emerald Spreadwing   *Lestes dryas*

BLUETS
__Taiga Bluet   *Coenagrion resolutum*
__Arroyo Bluet   *Enallagma praevarum*
__River Bluet   *Enallagma anna*
__Familiar Bluet   *Enallagma civile*
__Tule Bluet   *Enallagma carunculatum*
__Alkali Bluet   *Enallagma clausum*
__Northern Bluet   *Enallagma annexum*
__Boreal Bluet   *Enallagma boreale*
__Rainbow Bluet   *Enallagma antennatum*
__Double-striped Bluet   *Enallagma basidens*
__Orange Bluet   *Enallagma signatum*

DAMSELFLIES — continued

FORKTAILS
__Pacific Forktail   *Ischnura cervula*

__Plains Forktail   *Ischnura damula*

__Western Forktail   *Ischnura perparva*

__Eastern Forktail   *Ischnura verticalis*

__Western Red Damsel   *Amphiagrion abbreviatum*

DANCERS
__Blue-fronted Dancer   *Argia apicalis*

__Paiute Dancer   *Argia alberta*

__Variable Dancer   *Argia fumipennis*

__Vivid Dancer   *Argia vivida*

__Emma's Dancer   *Argia emma*

INDEX OF SPECIES